DA
OUT
WITH KIDS
IN THE MIDLANDS

CW01507047

DEDICATED TO

EMILY, JACK, NELL AND GUY

THANK YOU

DAYS OUT

WITH KIDS

IN THE MIDLANDS

TRIED-AND-TESTED
FUN FAMILY OUTINGS

Deborah Castle
Jane Lockley

BON•BON
PUBLISHING

FIRST PUBLISHED IN 2001 BY
BON•BON PUBLISHING
24 ENDLESHAM ROAD
LONDON SW12 8JU

COPYRIGHT © BON•BON PUBLISHING 2001
EXCEPT BEESTON CASTLE REPORT © CHRISTINA MAY

COVER PHOTOGRAPHS:
FRONT COVER © BON•BON PUBLISHING 2001/JONATHAN PERUGIA
BACK COVER © LLANGOLLEN WHARF AND © ASH END HOUSE FARM

ISBN   1-901411-34-6

SERIES EDITOR JANET BONTHRON
DESIGN BY CAROLINE GRIMSHAW
ILLUSTRATIONS BY SAM TOFT

PRINTED & BOUND
IN FINLAND BY
WS BOOKWELL, JUVA

Contents

Animal Encounters

Look! Look! Look!

The Great Outdoors

Somewhat Historical

Up, Down, There & Back

The Sun Has Got His Hat On

Introduction

WELCOME TO DAYS OUT WITH KIDS, WRITTEN FOR PEOPLE
with children in the Midlands. Now in its fifth
edition, the book is packed with ideas for fun family
outings. With lots of outings to try and updated
information, I hope that it will help you tackle some
of those perennial problems:

WHAT ARE WE GOING TO DO TODAY?
As a mother of four children, I know how important
it is to get out of the house some days. Equally, how
difficult it can be to think of places to go for a
change; places that are not too far; where everyone
can have a good time; where young children will be
well catered for. This book gives you a personal
selection of great outings to choose from; if you go
out on one or two a month, there are well over a
year's worth of different trips inside!

BUT WHERE IS REALLY GOOD?
Often these days it is not a problem knowing about
places to go, but rather whether those places will
really be a good trip for people with children. If
you've no time to sift through leaflets, or don't know
anyone who's been themselves then it can be
daunting to try something new. The outings featured
in Days Out With Kids have all been done personally,
by mothers with children in tow. They are all tried-
and-tested recommended trips: we've been there
ourselves!

WHAT ABOUT MUMS AND DADS TOO?
If the prospect of yet another adventure playground
bores you, then you'll welcome something different.
Our aim has been to describe outings enjoyed by
everyone in the family, with something to appeal to
adults as well as children. Some of the trips may
look like just adult outings, but they're not. We want
to introduce you to some of the unusual and fun

places we have been to. You may all get something different out of the day, but that doesn't matter, as long as you all have a good time.

HOW ARE PLACES SELECTED FOR THE BOOK?

We have included a variety of trips: for the winter and the summer, for rain and sunshine, some nearby, some a greater distance. Some of the trips are old favourites, many times visited. Others were suggested by friends as places that they love. We have noted what childcare facilities are provided in each case: pushchair accessibility, high chairs, nappy tables etc., but haven't selected places purely on this basis. Rather, the facilities information is given on the principle that if you know in advance what is provided you can plan your day accordingly.

All trips were done anonymously. No one has paid to be included in the book, and the views and opinions expressed are very much personal thoughts and reactions. Places are in the book because we had a good time there, and think that other people with children could too.

WHAT AGES OF CHILDREN ARE COVERED?

The book is aimed at people with babies, toddlers and school-aged children. Many of the trips will also appeal to children up to early teens, and, of course, adults too!

The facts given for each outing have been checked rigorously. However, things do change, and please check details (particularly opening times) before you set out.

JANET BONTHRON
SERIES EDITOR
BON•BON VENTURES
24 ENDLESHAM ROAD
LONDON SW12 8JU

How To Use This Book

EACH SECTION OF THE BOOK COVERS TRIPS WHICH FALL INTO the same broad category of attraction. Outings are described alphabetically within the section. If you know what sort of outing you want to do, then just look at the section titles, read the section summaries below, and flick through the entries included in that section. Alternatively, the handy planning guide is a rapid, self-explanatory table for identifying the right trip for you.

 ANIMAL ENCOUNTERS covers trips to farms, zoos and other birds and beasties type places. Children and animals are a winning combination, and there are plenty of places around the Midlands which offer it. We have chosen those which we think are distinctive in some way, for example superb handling opportunities for children, wonderful setting, or unusual or imaginatively-displayed animals.

 LOOK! LOOK! LOOK! features places with exhibitions or displays which children should particularly enjoy, be they of aeroplanes (Birmingham Airport or Cosford), cars (Midland Motor Museum), or chocolates (Cadbury World). These outings offer the chance for children to see something unusual or to experience at close quarters something they may only have seen on television.

 THE GREAT OUTDOORS is about trips which are all or mostly outdoors in character, in an especially beautiful or quiet setting. Ideal for walks and strolls,

with plenty to see for adults whilst the kids run around exhausting themselves. Couldn't be better!

SOMEWHAT HISTORICAL attractions all have a bygone age theme. Your children may not fully appreciate the historical connotations, but will be able to enjoy the setting and exhibits, whilst you can wallow in romantic nostalgia!

UP, DOWN, THERE & BACK has steam train and canal ride outings. Puffs of steam and the smell of smoke in the air are always thrilling and the ones we have included have features which make them particularly accessible. Eat your heart out, Thomas the Tank Engine!

THE SUN HAS GOT HIS HAT ON includes picnic spots that are obviously just a small selection of what is available. Most good picnic spots tend to be closely guarded secrets, but these are ones which are favourites of ours. There is something about spreading your blanket on the ground and unpacking boxes and plates of picnic food that is just pure summertime, and you can't beat it. Happy munching! Of course, many of the locations in the previous sections are also excellent picnic spots.

IF YOU DON'T MIND WHAT SORT OF ATTRACTION YOU GO TO, BUT have other criteria (such as the weather, distance, or means of transport for example) which you need to satisfy, then the best way to use the book is to refer to the map and planning guide given on the following pages. These should help you to pick a suitable day out.

THE PLANNING GUIDE can help you select an outing by distance, prevailing weather, admittance to dogs, accessibility by public transport, or opening hours.

* **Free**, or particularly **good value**, trips are asterisked (£12.00 or less for a family of four).

Distances are approximate, and taken from Birmingham. We have erred on the generous side when deciding on the **wet weather** suitability – if there is somewhere to duck inside during an occasional shower then we say 'yes' under the wet weather trip heading. 'No' means, in our view, it would really be quite a miserable trip if it is raining. For people with **dogs**, 'yes' may mean on a lead only, so always take a lead.

With **public transport** accessibility we have indicated what is available, but you may need to do a short walk too in some cases. 'None' or 'limited' means that it would really be hard work going there without a car.

The planning guide also indicates whether **opening** periods are restricted (i.e. if a place is not open all the year, and/or only on some days of the week). For attractions cited as 'all year' opening, this excludes Christmas Day, Boxing Day and New Year's Day, so check if you want to go these days.

Once you have identified a trip that sounds appealing, refer to the detailed description for further information. Page numbers are given in the Planning Guide. The Fact File which accompanies each entry gives the address and telephone number, travel directions and distances, opening times and prices, and an indication of specific facilities (high chairs, nappy change areas, and eating places). Where appropriate, the Fact File also suggests other nearby attractions.

Map

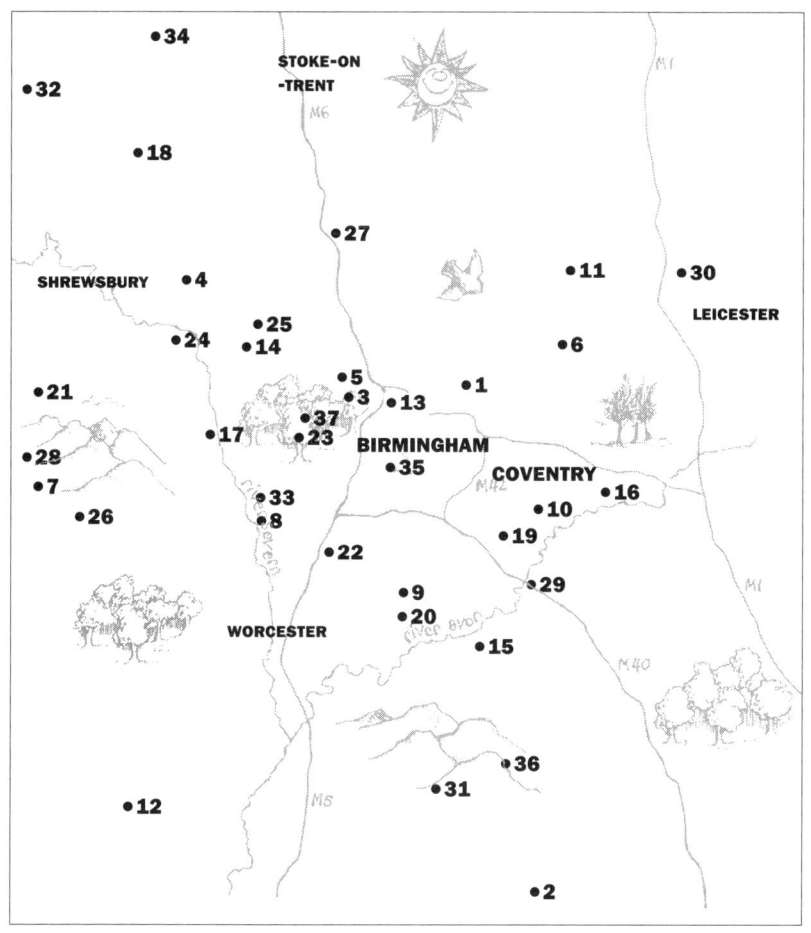

STOKE-ON
-TRENT

SHREWSBURY

LEICESTER

BIRMINGHAM

COVENTRY

WORCESTER

Planning Guide

OUTING	DISTANCE (MILES)	WET WEATHER TRIP	DOGS	PUBLIC TRANSPORT	OPEN	PAGE
ANIMAL ENCOUNTERS						
ASH END HOUSE CHILDRENS' FARM*	15	YES	NO	NONE	ALL YEAR	15
COTSWOLD WILDLIFE PARK	60	NO	YES	NONE	ALL YEAR	18
DUDLEY ZOO & CASTLE	10	NO	NO	BUS	ALL YEAR	21
HOO FARM ANIMAL KINGDOM	35	NO	NO	NONE	RESTRICTED	24
SANDWELL PARK FARM*	4	NO	NO	BUS	ALL YEAR	27
TWYCROSS ZOO	30	YES	NO	NONE	ALL YEAR	30
WERNLAS RARE POULTRY COLLECTION*	50	NO	YES	NONE	RESTRICTED	33
WEST MIDLAND SAFARI & LEISURE PARK	20	YES	NO	NONE	RESTRICTED	36
LOOK! LOOK! LOOK!						
COUGHTON COURT	15	YES	NO	BUS	RESTRICTED	39
COVENTRY AIRPORT - MIDLAND AIR MUSEUM*	25	YES	YES	BUS	ALL YEAR	42
DISCOVERY PARK, SNIBSTON	30	YES	NO	NO	ALL YEAR	45
NATIONAL BIRDS OF PREY CENTRE	60	NO	NO	NO	RESTRICTED	48
NATIONAL SEALIFE CENTRE	0	YES	NO	YES	ALL YEAR	51
RAF MUSEUM COSFORD*	20	YES	NO	NONE	ALL YEAR	54
THE SHIRE HORSE CENTRE	30	NO	YES	NONE	RESTRICTED	57
THE GREAT OUTDOORS						
COOMBE ABBEY COUNTRY PARK*	20	YES	YES	BUS	ALL YEAR	60
DUDMASTON*	40	YES	YES	BUS	RESTRICTED	63
HAWKSTONE PARK*	50	NO	YES	NONE	RESTRICTED	66
KENILWORTH*	25	NO	YES	BUS	ALL YEAR	69
RAGLEY HALL	20	NO	YES	BUS	RESTRICTED	72

OUTING	DISTANCE (MILES)	WET WEATHER TRIP	DOGS	PUBLIC TRANSPORT	OPEN	PAGE
SOMEWHAT HISTORICAL						
ACTON SCOTT HISTORIC WORKING FARM*	60	NO	NO	NONE	RESTRICTED	75
AVONCROFT MUSEUM OF HISTORIC BUILDINGS	20	YES	YES	TRAIN	RESTRICTED	78
THE BLACK COUNTRY LIVING MUSEUM	5	YES	NO	TRAIN & BUS	RESTRICTED	81
BLISTS HILL VICTORIAN TOWN	40	YES	YES	BUS	ALL YEAR	84
BOSCOBEL HOUSE AND MOSELEY OLD HALL	20	YES	NO	NONE	RESTRICTED	87
LUDLOW CASTLE*	50	YES	YES	TRAIN	RESTRICTED	90
SHUGBOROUGH FARM & ESTATE	20	YES	NO	NONE	RESTRICTED	93
STOKESAY CASTLE*	50	YES	NO	BUS	RESTRICTED	96
WARWICK CASTLE	20	YES	NO	TRAIN	ALL YEAR	99
UP, DOWN, THERE & BACK						
GREAT CENTRAL RAILWAY	45	YES	YES	TRAIN	RESTRICTED	102
THE GLOUCESTERSHIRE & WARWICKSHIRE RAILWAY	50	YES	YES	BUS	RESTRICTED	105
LLANGOLLEN WHARF & STEAM RAILWAY	75	YES	YES	NONE	RESTRICTED	108
SEVERN VALLEY RAILWAY	15	YES	YES	TRAIN	RESTRICTED	111
THE SUN HAS GOT HIS HAT ON						
BEESTON CASTLE*	60	NO	YES	NONE	ALL YEAR	114
THE BIRMINGHAM BOTANICAL GARDENS	1	NO	NO	BUS	ALL YEAR	117
BROADWAY TOWER COUNTRY PARK*	50	NO	YES	BUS	RESTRICTED	120
HIMLEY PARK & HALL*	15	NO	YES	TRAIN & BUS	ALL YEAR	123

SEE **HOW TO USE THIS GUIDE** FOR EXPLANATIONS

The sign in the illustration reads: "Please TAKE CARE WHILST FEEDING THE ANIMALS"

Animal Encounters

Ash End House Childrens' Farm

ASH END HOUSE FARM HAS LONG BEEN ONE OF OUR FAMILY'S favourite days out. Specifically designed to appeal to children, you can visit regularly throughout the year without tiring of it, and experience life on a working farm. We went recently with eighteen-month-old triplets, and their opinion was a resounding thumbs up! It is a real hands-on attraction though: don't expect to stand back and admire the animals, as here you have to get your hands dirty (and feet and trousers!).

"Children are able to go and collect an egg from the hen house"

Children can get fully involved with all the animals, ranging from huge Shire horses to tiny chicks, and from friendly Jersey cows to greedy goats. Many are kept undercover in pens and all can be seen easily by even the smallest child in a pushchair.

As you go in children are given a bucket of feed to take round. There is plenty of encouragement to get in with the animals and you will be readily relieved of your food supplies by keen lambs, goats or rabbits. Anything that thinks it needs feeding can be fed. Most of the animals are very tame, considering what they have to contend with, although one lively rabbit made a bid for freedom behind the straw bales when we last went.

In spring and summer you can help bottle feed the lambs and kid goats too.

The hatchery is always a treat. We've spent many an afternoon waiting "just for a few minutes while that cracked egg hatches" Be warned – it takes longer than you think, so it is probably best to pop in at the outset of your visit and come back again a few hours later to check progress. We have been rewarded on several occasions by seeing chicks hatch out. Children can also cuddle a newborn chick or duckling which always causes much delight.

Following on

Sam

from the hatchery are the most smelly pig sties any child could hope for. Home to some pretty substantial Saddleback pigs who never fail to amuse, it is usually a part of the visit where we don't linger!

For paying children the admission charge includes a pony ride. You may want to take a hat for this, as they are not provided.

The paths around the farm are well-made and fine for pushchairs but do tend to get messy especially at wet times of the year. If you do manage to forget wellies, don't despair as there is a Welly Shed where you may borrow a pair for your visit.

There is a picnic area overlooking the paddocks, and an excellent modern play area. There is also a cafeteria offering a good selection of snacks, meals and drinks. A final piece of advice – don't miss the piglet playlets or the wool spinning demonstrations most Sundays!

Fact File

- ADDRESS: Ash End House Farm, Middleton Lane, Middleton, near Tamworth, Staffordshire
- TELEPHONE: 0121 329 3240
- WEBSITE: www.ashendhouse.fsnet.co.uk
- DIRECTIONS: M42 junction 9, take the A4091 towards Tamworth Follow signs from A4091
- PUBLIC TRANSPORT: None
- DISTANCE: 15 miles
- TRAVEL TIME: 30 minutes
- OPENING: Daily 10.00am-5.00pm or dusk in winter
- PRICES: Adults £1.80, children £3.60
- RESTAURANT FACILITIES: Yes
- NAPPY CHANGING FACILITIES: Yes
- HIGH CHAIRS: Yes
- DOGS: No
- PUSHCHAIR-FRIENDLY: Yes
- NEARBY: Tamworth Castle (01827 63563) with period rooms, haunted bedroom and riverside gardens

Cotswold Wildlife Park

COME HERE TO SEE WILD ANIMALS THAT YOU CAN'T SEE ON A farm – real lions, rhinos and zebras to name a few, in 120 acres of gardens and landscaped parkland around a large Gothic-style manor house. It offers a varied, exciting day out and is just as much fun in winter as summer.

On arrival we headed straight for the real wild animals: the leopards, lions and rhinos. Well-signposted paths radiate out from the car park, so you can easily work out which way to go. On the way we admired the giant tortoises: huge boulders which unexpectedly started walking towards us. Despite wanting to ride on them, our daughter was tempted away with promises of more to come.

After a short walk past a vast, empty field we came to the zebra house, leopard house, and most spectacularly the lions.

"The lions were prowling around outside looking highly ferocious"

Obviously zebras and leopards aren't stupid (it was a cold day) as they were all inside, but the large glass windows in their houses, with steps up for children, meant we could all get a wonderful view of them. The lions were prowling around looking highly ferocious, but the close up sight of those sharp yellow teeth, glinting eyes and huge paws (even safely behind wire netting) proved too much for our daughter and we had to beat a hasty retreat to the relative safety of the Bactrian camels.

Back around the manor house there are plenty more animals to see – red pandas, monkeys, gibbons and emus are just some of what is on offer. They are all well-displayed, with ditches and viewing

platforms enabling you to get a really close-up look. To be within six foot of a white rhino is quite an experience and our son was clearly enthralled, although we were not able to persuade him that it wasn't a "dawg"! There is also a children's farmyard area, with a good display of pot-bellied pigs, angora goats, rabbits, guinea pigs, ducks and poultry. Some of these may be stroked and petted, and they are all accessible for small children to see and appreciate.

The manor house and attached buildings contain a number of other attractions, including the reptile and invertebrate houses. Warm, with subdued lighting and suitably impressive slimies and slitheries, these proved very popular, although children have to be lifted to see inside some displays. The bat house, where you can look down on the bats swirling below you, was fascinating. It adjoins the glass animal house, where you can see a myriad of miniature glass animals both on display and being made. Alongside the reptile house is a new enclosure of Siamang gibbens, with both indoor and outdoor quarters.

Other areas to visit are the walled garden with otters, meerkats, penguins, and hornbills. Many more birds, including flamingos, cranes, swans and ducks can be seen in the lake area. You may not feed them though. All the paths are easily accessible to pushchairs, including those round the lake, and there are plenty of good, clear information boards and signs.

Behind the manor house you'll find an adventure playground with slides, swings, climbing equipment and other amusements for children from babyhood to at least eight-years-old. The helter-skelter is quite awe-inspiring and very popular with five-year-olds. The playground may get crowded in busy periods.

There is also a narrow gauge railway which runs at 20-minute intervals and takes you on a short tour of the whole park past most of the animals' enclosures (£1.00 adults, 50p children).

The park is well-served with picnic areas, with a large picnic lawn in front of the manor house, and picnic tables in several other locations, including the adventure playground. There is a large self-service cafe with some entertaining marmoset. During the summer there are many special events, including birds of prey flying demonstrations and snake handling days (first Sunday in the month).

Fact File

- ADDRESS: Cotswold Wildlife Park, Burford, Oxfordshire
- TELEPHONE: 01993 823006
- WEBSITE: www.cotswoldwildlifepark.co.uk
- DIRECTIONS: M40 to junction 15, then A429 to Stow on the Wold, and A424 to Burford. Signposted from Burford
- PUBLIC TRANSPORT: None
- DISTANCE: 60 miles
- TRAVEL TIME: 1 hour 30 minutes
- OPENING: Daily 10.00am-5.00pm or dusk, whichever earlier
- PRICES: £6.50 adults, £4.00 children, under-3's free
- RESTAURANT FACILITIES: Yes
- NAPPY CHANGING FACILITIES: Yes
- HIGH CHAIRS: Yes
- DOGS: Yes
- PUSHCHAIR-FRIENDLY: Yes
- NEARBY: Cotswolds Motor Museum and Toy Collection at Bourton-On-The-Water (01451 821255)

Dudley Zoo & Castle

COME TO DUDLEY TO SEE WILD ANIMALS AT CLOSE QUARTERS, amidst very pleasant wooded surroundings. Overlooked by the Castle, which may also be visited, there is more than enough for a whole day out. However, be warned, the site is on a hill, and although it offers the chance of some great views, some uphill buggy pushing cannot really be avoided!

The route up from the entrance is lined with owl enclosures and our game of 'spot the owl' just about worked in persuading our truculent toddler to walk up the fairly steep hill. Instead of wanting to be picked up, he ran from cage to cage trying to be the first to spot the sleeping owls hidden amongst the branches. There is a free chair lift to the top of the hill, but this is unsuitable for pushchairs and is only in operation in school holidays. If you really can't face the walk on a hot day though, there is a land train (free) which will take you on a quick 10-minute tour of the zoo and drop you at the top. The train has a special trailer to put (folded) pushchairs on.

> "The castle courtyard is a perfect spot for picnics and for playing knights and horses"

Having climbed that first steep hill, the paths level off and wind their way around all the different animals in enclosures. Most enclosures have fences which allow small children to see in, but some are down steps and those in pushchairs need to be lifted out to see. Do explore and wander, though, as despite several flights of steps, all the enclosures can be reached via pathways (apart from one area at the back which is clearly signposted as unsuitable for buggies).

Our Jungle Book crazy kids were delighted to meet 'Shere Khan' and his tiger cubs, found the new chimp house with the antics of the inhabitants hilarious, and were thrilled by the sheer size of the giraffes. The Asiatic lions are quite something, too. And so the visit continued; excitement at seeing one animal being surpassed by the excitement of seeing another and another . . . . Make your way round and up to the Discovery Centre where there are regular talks and sessions with animals.

The grounds are lovely and there are several picnic areas scattered about, with tables and benches. Half way round is a small indoor play area for under-fives, which has climbing apparatus and rocking horses, all on a wood-chip base.

Slowly wend your way up to the top of the hill, where you will come to the castle ruins: external walls, a keep, and a large grassy courtyard. The courtyard has benches, and is a perfect spot for picnics and for playing knights and horses once you've finished your sandwiches. There are even knightly litter bins!

You can climb up a spiral staircase to the top of the keep and peer through the turrets at marvellous views. We counted 57 steps. Back at ground level there are several ruined rooms to explore, and don't miss the light and music display in the Visitor Centre, which realistically depicts a year in the life of the people who lived in and around the castle in Medieval times. Our toddler found some of the life-sized characters rather too sinister, but the display is interactive, so you can come in and out as you want. If it gets too much for the imagination, escape into the sunshine outside!

The trip back down from the castle is much easier than the climb up and during school holidays there is a mini fun fair at the bottom of the hill with roundabouts and swing-boats. This gives a good opportunity to let off steam before getting back into the car.

A final point: don't miss the car park entrance as you arrive. It is poorly signposted and basically a dirt track!

Fact File

- ADDRESS: Dudley Zoo & Castle, 2 The Broadway, Dudley, West Midlands
- TELEPHONE: 01384 215300
- WEBSITE: www.dudleyzoo.org.uk
- DIRECTIONS: M5 junction 2 towards Dudley; zoo is situated just outside the town off the A461
- PUBLIC TRANSPORT: Buses to Dudley from Birmingham (74, 87, 120, 124, 126 and 140), then a 2-minute walk from bus station
- DISTANCE: 10 miles
- TRAVEL TIME: 30 minutes
- OPENING: Daily 10.00am-4.30pm (summer) or 3.30pm (winter)
- PRICES: Adults £6.75, children £4.50, under-4's free, family £23.00
- RESTAURANT FACILITIES: Yes
- NAPPY CHANGING FACILITIES: Yes
- HIGH CHAIRS: Yes
- DOGS: No
- PUSHCHAIR-FRIENDLY: Yes
- NEARBY: Wren's Nest Nature Reserve, a 1-mile trail from the Caves pub, or Merryhill Shopping Centre for indoor shops

Hoo Farm Animal Kingdom

With a moo-moo here, and a moo-moo there

OLD MACDONALD HAD A FARM, BUT HIS DIDN'T HAVE ostriches, deer and llamas. Hoo Farm has, and more besides. This is a farm with traditional animals, some more unusual breeds, and several extras on top, both indoors and out, which make it a good choice for an action-packed day.

At the entrance the children were immediately drawn to the undercover tractor race track: a converted barn with loads of pedal tractors on a mini grand-prix circuit. There are junior Quad bikes available too, and a junior rifle range, both for 6 to 9-year-olds, and for an extra charge (£1.00 per child each). New last year was the craft area with candle dipping, glass and pottery painting, so there is lots to keep you busy

"If you visit the farm as Christmas approaches you can choose a tree"

We dragged them away from all that with promises to return later and made a start in the farmyard. Here we found rabbits, racoons (asleep), and hens roaming around. On through the wildlife area there are more rabbits, owls and birds to be seen. But when you leave the farmyard, have your bags of food (50p a bag from the entrance) at the ready. First to the fence were the goats: clambering up, putting their faces into ours, demanding food, but they are very gentle and ate from our hands. Next, "a camel", according to our three-year-old, in fact, a llama called Lancelot who soon was feeding hungrily from our hands, closely followed by the deer.

The trail is well laid-out, so that there is always something new to see. The different animals are housed close together and there isn't time for little ones to get bored, nor do they realise how far they are walking. Paths are easily negotiated with a pushchair too.

Carrying on our way, we came across a huge beehive: in fact a building with a glass-sided beehive inside, letting you see the bees at work on their honeycomb. Next was the Vietnamese pot-bellied pig, snoring in the sunshine, and then the hen house. As we approached, the hens came running from all directions. A few handfuls of food later we went into the Egg Experience – an undercover area where we learnt all about egg growth and found some of our own warm eggs to take home!

The next part of the walk is dedicated to the Christmas tree story. For a while animals disappear from the trail and instead you amble through a pine wood. If you visit the farm as Christmas approaches you can choose a tree to buy from the many hundreds growing on the farm. Be careful of nettles in the forest, though, it would be easy for little legs to be stung.

Once out of the pine wood, we were back to the animals. Sheep, this time. Then on through the Wild Wood of Wind in the Willows (adapted!), a quick play in Toad Hall, past some pigs and then face to face with the enormous farm bull. We hurried on as the Sheep Racing began – for a small fee you can be the 'owner' of a sheep and walk away with a rosette if it wins. It is on every day except Fridays (April to September).

Horse and cart rides (50p) are available at some times, and there is a small play area where grown-ups can sit down alongside. You'll find picnic tables in here and also outside the barn. If the weather is poor there is an undercover play area, whilst the Cow Shed Tea Room offers drinks, snacks and hot rolls.

Fact File

● ADDRESS: Hoo Farm Animal Kingdom, Preston-on-the-Weald Moors, Telford, Shropshire
● TELEPHONE: 01952 677917
● WEBSITE: www.virtual-shropshire.co.uk/hoofarm
● DIRECTIONS: M54 to Junction 4, follow the B5060 (signposted to Donnington from the motorway) over three roundabouts. The farm is signposted from the next roundabout
● PUBLIC TRANSPORT: None
● DISTANCE: 35 miles
● TRAVEL TIME: 1 hour
● OPENING: Daily 10.00am-6.00pm March to September, and December
● PRICES: Adults £3.95, children £2.95, family £14.00, under-2's froo
● RESTAURANT FACILITIES: Yes
● NAPPY CHANGING FACILITIES: Yes
● HIGH CHAIRS: Yes
● DOGS: No
● PUSHCHAIR-FRIENDLY: Yes
● NEARBY: Telford Town Park, a parkland area with speciality gardens

Sandwell Park Farm

Sandwell Park Farm is situated in the Sandwell Valley, an area of woodland on the outskirts of West Bromwich. Although within a stone's throw of the M5 motorway, it is a peaceful reconstruction of a 19th century farm with traditional farming methods and breeds. Look out for craft fairs and other events on Bank Holidays, and the Sandwell Show in August.

As we approached the farm two large, brown horses trotted by in a nearby field, and as most young children love to see animals close up, we knew we were in for a good visit.

There are two exhibitions just inside the entrance: a Victorian street scene, and 'People of the Valley' – life sized reconstructions showing inhabitants in the Sandwell Valley from stone-aged hunter gatherers through to medieval monks and the 18th century. The small exhibitions provide lots to talk about with children. Ours thought the monks were so good that we had to go and see them three

"Some sties have steps so that children can peer in to watch the sleeping pigs"

times, and listen to the gregorian chants, or "the monk music" as they called it. (To avoid the steps down to the exhibitions use the door half way down the building).

Through the exhibitions, you then enter the main farmyard. Watch where you are walking at this point. This is a working farm, and some of the animals will have passed through the farmyard on their way to the fields. You'll find turkeys, chickens and ducks roaming freely around, and lining the outside of the farmyard are the stalls for cows. These were in the fields when we went, but you can go into the fields

and see them at close quarters.

The cows may have been in the fields, but the Tamworth pigs weren't! The smell on a hot summer's day is quite something, but the children enjoyed shouting "Poohy" as they pushed their faces close to the bars of the stalls. Some sties have steps so that children can peer in to watch the sleeping pigs, but you will have to do some lifting. It may be busy during the week with school parties.

As well as the animals' stalls, there is also a barn, a pigeon loft and a granary to be seen. The pigeon loft and the granary are up a flight of wooden stairs. In the middle of the farmyard are some Victorian farm machinery and be prepared to answer "What's that for?" Luckily, there are lots of information boards about.

Don't miss the walled kitchen garden: a gardener's paradise, with fruits and vegetables growing in abundance, and a reconstructed Victorian fruit house. For our children, used to seeing

vegetables on plates, it was a revelation to see them actually growing on plants.

From the farm you can walk to the Priory itself, now just remains. There are several paths through the Sandwell Valley suitable for pushchairs and to get to the ruins you need to follow the bridle path over the M5 bridge. The walk takes about 45 minutes, but you could spend a lot longer exploring the valley.

There is a picnic area with plenty of large tables next to the farmyard. It is gravelled so watch out for scraped knees; also beware that toddlers don't squeeze past the rails of the small pond there. The nearby tea room serves drinks and snacks.

If you have any energy left, Dartmouth Park is on the left as you leave the farm. There are plenty of grassy areas, the usual swings and slides, and a paddling pool, filled during the summer to a depth of about 3", great for cooling tired feet on a hot day!

Fact File

- ● ADDRESS: Sandwell Park Farm, Sandwell Valley Country Park, Salters Lane, West Bromwich, West Midlands
- ● TELEPHONE: 0121 553 0220
- ● DIRECTIONS: Follow signs from junction 1 of the M5 and West Bromwich town centre
- ● PUBLIC TRANSPORT: Bus to West Bromwich (0121 200 2700 for times), 1-mile walk through Sandwell Centre and Dartmouth Park to farm. Signposted
- ● DISTANCE: 4 miles
- ● TRAVEL TIME: 30 minutes
- ● OPENING: 10.00am-4.30pm daily
- ● PRICES: Free during the week. £1.00 adults, 50p children at weekends, under-5's free
- ● RESTAURANT FACILITIES: Yes
- ● NAPPY CHANGING FACILITIES: Yes
- ● HIGH CHAIRS: Yes
- ● DOGS: No
- ● PUSHCHAIR-FRIENDLY: Yes
- ● NEARBY: Forge Mill Farm interpretation centre (0121 588 7210) to see milking from 4.00pm-5.30pm

Twycross Zoo

A WONDERFUL SMALL ZOO AND CONSERVATION CENTRE, WHERE the animals are very accessible to children, and with lots going on, particularly in the summer, to make a full and exciting day out.

Most of the animals are captive bred, either at Twycross or another zoo, so because of the active breeding programme there is a good chance of seeing young animals on your visit. The breeding programme ranges from primates and parrots to less lovely giant spotted slugs, so a trip here will extend your knowledge of the whole of the animal kingdom.

The zoo is particularly good at introducing children to the smells (fruit bat cages – PHEW!), sounds (the howler moneys), and sights (lions' lunch) of real animals, rather than those on pictures or television. There are lots of demonstrations and chances to watch the daily routine of the zoo world: look out for the timetables on the blackboard at the information centre.

We headed straight for the Elephant House on arrival, in order to catch the feeding and nail cutting demonstration. Hurrying along, we were distracted momentarily by the leggy giraffes, whose stately size immediately impressed on the children that we were going to see some real animals. With promises of returning later, we eventually made it to the elephants.

"Don't miss Iris the elephant wolfing down entire loaves of bread, bananas (unskinned!) and whole cabbages"

Don't miss this one: the sight of Iris wolfing down entire loaves of bread, bananas (unskinned!) and whole cabbages will enthral any child, or adult for that matter. The way she delicately curled the end of

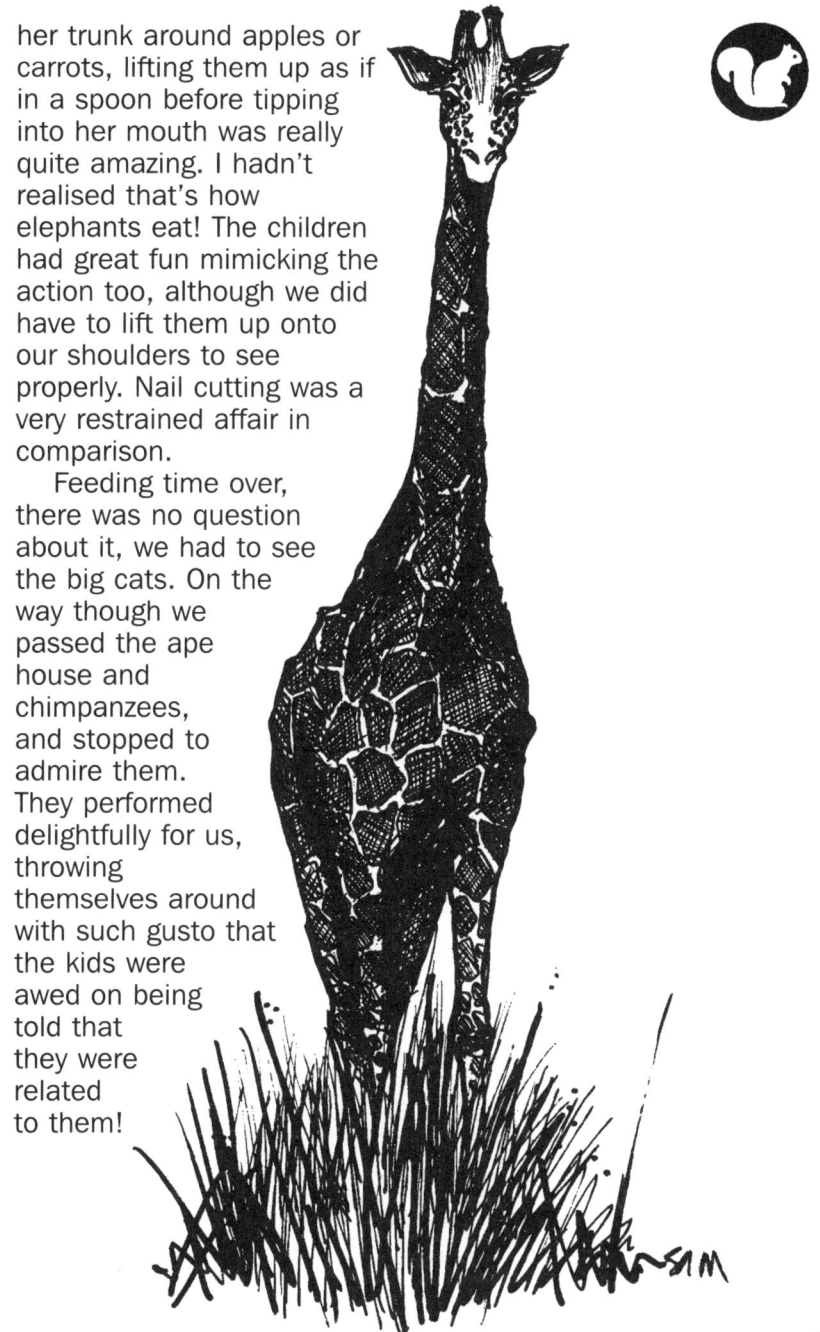

her trunk around apples or carrots, lifting them up as if in a spoon before tipping into her mouth was really quite amazing. I hadn't realised that's how elephants eat! The children had great fun mimicking the action too, although we did have to lift them up onto our shoulders to see properly. Nail cutting was a very restrained affair in comparison.

Feeding time over, there was no question about it, we had to see the big cats. On the way though we passed the ape house and chimpanzees, and stopped to admire them. They performed delightfully for us, throwing themselves around with such gusto that the kids were awed on being told that they were related to them!

You can get very close to the tigers prowling in their enclosure. That's if your children don't run away at the sight of them. They are such magnificent creatures that it is worth going back for a second look.

Plan your day around the demonstrations, or just wander round. Other than the elephants there is sea-lion, penguin and seal feeding daily (subject to circumstances), and lots of ad-hoc talks and displays. Everything is well-marked and easy to see. All the paths are fine for pushchairs, and the zoo is laid out such that you keep coming back to something recognisable before branching off somewhere new. It is just the right size not to be overwhelming and all the children's favourites are there.

During the summer there are donkey rides, train rides on a miniature railway or a small playground. There are plenty of picnic spots, where you can eat your sandwiches surrounded by the animals in adjoining fields. This is particularly useful, as it keeps everyone entertained as they eat.

Fact File

- ADDRESS: Twycross Zoo, Atherstone, Warwickshire
- TELEPHONE: 01827 880250/880440
- WEBSITE: www.tywcrosszoo.com
- DIRECTIONS: M42 north junction 11, onto the A444 towards Twycross. Signposted
- PUBLIC TRANSPORT: None
- DISTANCE: 30 miles
- TRAVEL TIME: 45 minutes
- OPENING: Daily, 10.00am-6.00pm (summer) or dusk (winter)
- PRICES: Adults £6.50, children £4.50, under-3's free
- RESTAURANT FACILITIES: Yes
- NAPPY CHANGING FACILITIES: Yes
- HIGH CHAIRS: Yes
- DOGS: No
- PUSHCHAIR-FRIENDLY: Yes
- NEARBY: Middleton Hall near Tamworth, Georgian hall and grounds, with adjacent craft centre (01827 283095)

Wernlas Rare Poultry Collection

Cackle, cackle Mother Goose
Have you any feathers loose?

RATHER OFF THE BEATEN TRACK, YOU WILL NOT COME UPON Wernlas by chance, but it is worth making the effort to find for a peaceful day out with plenty of hands-on encounters with animals.

Driving down endless country lanes to get there the children were delighted by all the tractors and other farm machines in the fields and on the roads. We would just squeeze past one, and another would appear. The final approach is up a one track lane, so be prepared to pull over if necessary onto a narrow verge as you climb the hill.

The Collection was established in 1977 and now boasts over 80 different breeds of poultry, housed in runs spread over a meadow on the side of a wooded valley known as

"The children insisted on imitating every cock-a-doodle-doo"

The Dingle. As well as poultry, there are also rare breeds of sheep to see, and pigs, donkeys and goats all waiting to be patted and stroked by visitors.

For children, the chief attraction is the close contact with the animals. For 10p you can buy tubs of chicken feed, encouraging the children to go right up to the runs to feed the birds (as if they needed any encouragement). As well as the birds in runs, there are also hens which roam freely and children can hand-feed them, if they'll keep still long enough to tempt the birds to approach.

As the Collection breeds rare birds, there are

always chicks of varying ages to be seen. There are special living quarters for the youngest of the birds, visited with a member of the staff, who tells you about the different species and their stages of development. Children can hold these tiny balls of feathers in their hands. Only our older child was willing to have a go, but dropped his chick because "it stabbed me"! However, he was encouraged to try again by the staff who are used to this kind of thing no doubt.

We spent the first part of our visit looking round the chicken runs, a colourful and noisy experience, particularly as our children insisted on imitating every cock-a-doodle-doo. The field is rather uneven and on the side of a hill, but it's nevertheless

manageable for a pushchair, although if the ground were wet, it might be a little more difficult. If you plan to visit after a period of wet weather, wellies would be a must.

There are two picnic areas on the site; one on the slopes of the valley, or one outside the refreshment cabin. Here you can buy drinks and snacks or you can eat your own food.

Picnic over, it was off to see the other animals. You are encouraged to go in and make a fuss of the goats and donkeys and to get as close as you wish to the sheep and pigs. Beware of the goats though, they will eat anything, including children's clothes!

Before we left we sat on a bench and had a last look round. As usual, it was the pigs and piglets that had most fascinated the children, apparently because they were "just like Pigling Bland". With animals and humans getting the chance to mingle in close proximity here, you'll understand the comparison.

Fact File

● ADDRESS: Wernlas Rare Poultry Collection, Green Lane, Onibury, near Ludlow, Shropshire
● TELEPHONE: 01584 856318
● DIRECTIONS: Just off the A49 between Shrewsbury and Ludlow. Signposted from Onibury
● PUBLIC TRANSPORT: None
● DISTANCE: 50 miles
● TRAVEL TIME: 1 hour
● OPENING: 10.30am-5.30pm Tuesday to Sunday and BH Mondays. Other Mondays from mid July to mid September only
● PRICES: Adults £3.00, children £1.50, under-4's free
● RESTAURANT FACILITIES: Limited (summer)
● NAPPY CHANGING FACILITIES: No
● HIGH CHAIRS: No
● DOGS: Yes
● PUSHCHAIR-FRIENDLY: Yes
● NEARBY: Hopton Castle, ruins of Norman castle near Craven Arms

West Midland Safari & Leisure Park

ONE DAY DOESN'T SEEM ENOUGH TO SEE AND DO ALL THAT there is here, so leave yourself plenty of time. Getting in can be a slow process on a busy day, but as we waited there were already squeals of delight coming from the back of the car as camels were spotted on the horizon. This set the tone for the next 90 minutes' journey through the wild lands of three continents, with shouts of "Look, tigers!" or "Mummy, zebras!" whenever we went over the next hill or round the next bend.

The Park is split into African, American and Eurasian sections and within these are areas where you can drive with your car windows open. There are even some areas where you can feed the animals through your open window. There are, however, other areas where opening your windows is definitely not allowed. Make sure you do a toilet stop before you start on the drive!

"A friendly camel put his head inside the car to say hello"

The lion enclosures are the first of these 'strictly out-of-bounds' areas. As you go through electronically controlled double gates there is a feeling of adventure, and the adrenaline flows as you realise that you will be separated from the lions only by your car door. It feels uncanny to be braking to avoid a lioness wandering across the road, but for children, it is a marvellous opportunity to come face to face with what they have so far seen only in picture books.

After the perils of the lions, we opened the car windows again to be greeted by a friendly camel, who put his head inside to say hello. The children loved it, but mummy was a bit startled to almost have a face wash from a large tongue!

Then came rhinoceroses, zebras, cows with enormous horns (Ankole Cattle) and peacocks (actually emus, but our children had never seen an emu before). All thrilling to see in a natural setting.

Another treat was the tigers, who decided to have an argument as we drove past and were roaring and running around. We were grateful here that they were safely enclosed.

"Bambi's daddy!" shouted the children as we entered the final drive-through section. Here, the deer roam freely and are quick to put their heads into the car in search of food. If you want to make the most of this, be sure to buy a packet of food (£1.25) as you enter the Park, but be prepared! They are determined and it was difficult to drive away once they had got their head inside the car.

The rest of the Park is a fun fair and an area more like a traditional zoo, with a reptile house, monkeys in cages and an animal encounters area.

The crocodiles and alligators in the reptile house were a magnet for our kids, with their glass-walled pools enabling you to see them amongst the fish.

Plan to see the sea-lions' act: four times a day in a specially built arena. There is also a parrot performance. The hippo feeding every afternoon is a riot: you can peer down at these lumbering giants from a viewing platform above the lake as they chomp their way through whole cabbages and the like. Check out the new Bat House and maze, planned for 2001. There are amusement rides to suit all ages, from gentle roundabouts to the stomach-churning pirate ship. Rides are an extra charge and you can buy a multi-ride wrist band (£7.00 or £5.00 for smaller kids) or individual tickets. There are several fast food kiosks and cafeterias.

On the way home a voice from the back of the car reminded us: "We didn't go on the train". Yes, we had missed the Safari Express which gives a (free) ride. But when you go in you are given a free return ticket to the Park. We'll definitely be using ours!

Fact File

- ADDRESS: West Midland Safari & Leisure Park, Spring Grove, Bewdley, Worcestershire
- TELEPHONE: 01299 404604
- WEBSITE: www.wmsp.co.uk
- DIRECTIONS: M5 junction 3 from the north and A456 towards Kidderminster, or junction 6 and A449. From Kidderminster follow the A456 towards Bewdley. Signposted
- PUBLIC TRANSPORT: None
- DISTANCE: 70 miles
- TRAVEL TIME: 1 hour 30 minutes
- OPENING: 17 March to end October daily 10.00 4.00pm
- PRICES: £5.95 per person, under-4's free. Includes free return visit
- RESTAURANT FACILITIES: Yes
- NAPPY CHANGING FACILITIES: Yes
- HIGH CHAIRS: Yes
- DOGS: No, bookable kennels available
- PUSHCHAIR-FRIENDLY: Yes
- NEARBY: Wrye Forest, west of Bewdley, with waymarked walks

Look! Look! Look!

Coughton Court

More than just a stately home, Coughton Court offers exhibitions on the gunpowder plot and children's clothes, picnic opportunities, riverside and lakeside walks, formal gardens and two churches to see. Everything is on a small scale: the grounds are not so extensive as to tire little legs and the exhibitions are just long enough to keep kids interested.

As we approached, shouts of "Look, a castle!" came from the back of the car, and indeed it did look like a castle, with turrets and a flag flying from the roof. The children were eager to get a closer look; and happily jumped out.

"With bonfire night in sight, the gunpowder plot exhibition was very popular"

You'll need to picnic before you go in, as picnics are not allowed in the grounds of the house. There is a special picnic area, though, close to the car park with plenty of tables and space for running round and playing. We started our visit in the stable yard. In the buildings lining the yard are exhibitions of the gunpowder plot and Victorian children's clothes, plus the restaurant. As we went towards the end of October, with bonfire night in sight, the gunpowder plot exhibition was very popular with our crew. It includes a written commentary and a video programme, and has poignant relevance to Coughton Court as two of the plotters were married to daughters of the house.

Next, the children's clothes which included both

formal and informal wear in the 19th century. Our children were more interested in the toys here, although they did comment on the christening gown, which they claimed to recognise from the photos of their own christenings!

As the exhibitions are small and quite crowded, it was then time for a run round, so we set out for a walk along the river and round the lake. The walk is easy to follow, but in places can be wet, so take wellies. There were no problems with the pushchair.

It's a very pleasant walk, with trees lining the sides of the river and branches overhead. We played our own version of Pooh Sticks, which involves dropping a stick into the river and seeing if we can keep sight of it as we walk along. There are no railings at the side of the river and the undergrowth makes it difficult in places to see where the edge of the river bank is, but if you keep to the paths there should be no problems. The path takes you around the lake which has some lovely ducks, some with amazing feather colours, and all very tame.

We called in on the two churches. These are like

any other small country church, but the kids were fascinated by the effigies of people apparently sleeping on top of the family vault.

Eventually, we made our way into the house itself. Pushchairs have to be left outside. Carrying the toddler, we noted the antlers adorning the walls of the entrance hall and the huge collection of pewter plates mounted on one of the walls: "What°a silly place to put plates", said our three-year-old. Although the house may be of limited interest for young children, older children would enjoy the Quiz Guide (60p). The tiger skin rug in one room was a highlight though, complete with claws, head and teeth, which the children thought was wonderful.

Outside the house, all that remained to be seen were the formal gardens, which looked and smelt lovely and had a fish pond. The newly created Rose Labyrinth, inspired by a ballad about Rosamund, mistress of Henry II, is a fun maze for children to end the day in.

Fact File

- ADDRESS: Coughton Court, Alcester, Warwickshire
- TELEPHONE: 01789 762435
- WEBSITE: www.nationaltrust.org.uk
- DIRECTIONS: A435 from Birmingham, or from M42 Junction 3 follow A435 towards Redditch. Signposted from Studley
- PUBLIC TRANSPORT: Midland Red bus 146 from Birmingham Bull Ring bus station. Hourly service, does not run Sundays (0121 200 2700)
- DISTANCE: 15 miles
- TRAVEL TIME: 25 minutes
- OPENING: Weekends 11.30-5.00pm 17 March to 28 October. Plus Easter Monday/Tuesday;Wednesdays to Fridays from 31 March to end of September; and all Tuesdays in August. Closed 23 June
- PRICES: House and grounds, adults £6.95, children £3.50, family £21.50, under-5's free. Reduced price for grounds only. National trust members free
- RESTAURANT FACILITIES: Yes
- NAPPY CHANGING FACILITIES: Yes
- HIGH CHAIRS: Yes
- DOGS: No
- PUSHCHAIR-FRIENDLY: Yes, except house
- NEARBY: Stratford on Avon, 10 miles away

Coventry Airport
Midland Air Museum

THE MIDLAND AIR MUSEUM AT COVENTRY AIRPORT IS ONE OF the most low key, delightful set ups we know. Just to the South of Coventry, off the A45 beside the airport, it is housed in a hangar of a building, unheated, no frills, and more helpful and charming staff you could not hope to meet. Set up in 1967 by a small group of local enthusiasts, and developed gradually to the present stage, the Museum is obviously a labour of love and devotion, with a very un-glitzy feel.

Your arrival is dominated by the classic, and awe-inspiring Vulcan, with its distinctive delta wing silhouette, setting the scene for your visit. Inside, the reception area is lined with every small boy's dream collection of model aircraft. A 5' long model of the USS Enterprise aircraft carrier was a particular irresistible source of fascination here.

"In the summer you can climb into the cockpits to try them out"

The display hall is full of real aircraft to admire and marvel at, some with steps up to peer into the cockpit, and some that you can actually climb into to get the genuine feeling of being a pilot. Even looking from the ground you can get a real feel for how claustrophobic it all was. A working model (with switches to fiddle with) of a cargo plane shows how the freight is loaded in and out. And there is a large collection of engines spanning a century of engine technology, all in various stages of assembly so that you can see exactly how they were developed. Buy the guide to help work out what everything is!

Coventry's part in WW2 is featured in the Whitley

Gallery, with log books of pilots, and the remains of a bomber. Fingers poking in bullet holes, we didn't need much of an imagination to picture what it was all like. Our boys (large and small) loved gloating over the vast collection of scale model aircraft of every sort. There is a junior model club which meets at the museum, so presumably the stock increases regularly. The Museum is staffed by volunteers, all enthusiastic and very knowledgeable. One was able to tell our 9-year-old all about the Vulcan and the nuclear missile it had carried – it all sounded frighteningly Heath Robinson to me!

On the grass outside stands a huge collection of planes of every description. We all loved climbing up the steps to look at the cockpits (very uncomfortable seats, we reckoned), seeing which ones had been restored and generally admiring their size and grace. They are all old aircraft, and in the summer you can climb into the cockpits to try them out for comfort. We spent some happy minutes climbing into the hold of the cargo plane, and from there up a rather scary 6' ladder into the cockpit. Not for the fainthearted, but worth it, just to be able to see the array of dials and switches that faced the pilots, not to mention the pathetically small sunshades to prevent dazzle.

The picnic tables are placed so that you can sit and watch the small (and occasionally larger) planes take off and land at Coventry Airport alongside the museum. This was one of the highlights of our visit, even in the depths of winter.

The coffee shop serves simple snacks and refreshments. It is all very clean and well-kept. The shop stocks kits and accessories as well as books, pictures and other relevant material.

Possibly not an outing for you if you don't have the faintest interest in planes, but well worth a visit with kids of about 6 upwards. Our 4-year-old loved the climbing around, but found it all a bit much after a short time. The bigger boys adored it and want to go back for another session in the summer. It is not a smart, or slick place, but the affection, knowledge and devotion of all involved shine through, and make for a very enjoyable visit. Try it!

Fact File

● ADDRESS: Midland Air Museum, Coventry Airport, Baginton, Warwickshire
● TELEPHONE: 02476 301033
● WEBSITE: midlandairmuseum@aol.com
● DIRECTIONS: Off A45, south of Coventry, follow signs to Airport, then to Museum
● PUBLIC TRANSPORT: Buses from Coventry
● DISTANCE: 25 miles
● TRAVEL TIME: 30-45 minutes
● OPENING: Daily 10.00am-5.00pm (to 4.30pm in winter and 6.00pm summer Sundays and Bank Holidays)
● PRICES: Adults £3.75, children £2.25, under-5's free
● RESTAURANT FACILITIES: Yes (snacks)
● NAPPY CHANGING FACILITIES: Due in 2001
● HIGH CHAIRS: Yes
● DOGS: On leads
● PUSHCHAIR-FRIENDLY: Yes
● NEARBY: Lunt Roman Fort, Baginton or Hatton Country World in Warwick

Discovery Park, Snibston

DEVELOPED AFTER THE LOCAL COLLIERY CLOSED DOWN IN THE mid-70s, Snibston is a mixture of open spaces, an outdoor science-based play area, former mine buildings plus a huge hall housing various science and museum galleries, shop, cafe and information centre. There is also a nature reserve on the site. You couldn't ask for more from a day out with your kids.

The main indoor attraction is the Science Alive! gallery, with endless displays and hands on experiments to illustrate every theory and principle you can imagine: from air pressure (floating a beach ball miraculously on a flow of air) to solar power or building electric circuits. We especially enjoyed riding a bike and driving the skeleton alongside it, seeing how our bones and joints work; and using the gadgets that

"You rarely see all the children in a place so totally involved"

let you look inside your own eyeball. Light, prisms, mirrors, every single aspect of science seems to be illustrated with clear, excellent experiments. In yet another section you can try your hand at signalling with semaphore flags, and the signs and symbols displays help to explain how various writing developed and how important symbols are in so many aspects of our life.

You rarely see all the children in a place so totally involved. I heard no moaning or grumbling whatever, and if yours are still going strong, but you need a pause, you can rest on a comfy seat in the Science Gallery, teasing your brain with some tabletop puzzles.

Outside the main gallery building is an outdoor science based play area with 15 big experiments bringing more principles to life. We built an arch bridge from foam blocks and all walked over it; made a huge block of iron swing to and fro using just a series of tiny pulls on a magnet; worked out how levers work; listened to a whisper from 150' away through a pair of "sound mirrors"; worked out some elementary principles of force and energy by swinging on a pair of linked swings. Everyone got something out of it, each taking it in at their own level.

From April to October the Wild Water area is open, where you can all have a happy time messing about with water flow: making dams, diverting a river, powering a water wheel and operating a flight of locks. Leave this until last rather than have people wandering round with wet sleeves!

The above ground tour of the old colliery buildings with an ex-miner guide was a suprise hit with our crew. We were told how the coal was mined, vivid stories of his time underground, and the dangers of working underground explained. The kids were gripped by it all and took a morbid interest in the fate of the canaries taken underground to detect carbon monoxide. The buildings are left almost exactly as they were when the mine closed, and the rather decrepit model people make a surreal contrast to the rest of the Science Park, with

its state of the art displays. The tours start every hour (small extra charge), and you should get your tickets as you arrive. At 1-hour long, under-7's will probably find the tour rather too much.

Towards the rear of the site, around 10 minutes walk from the main displays, is the Nature Reserve, a compact and interesting area with a well-signed trail around it. There are ponds, marshy areas, meadows and woodlands to look at with a nicely arranged picnic area. It is all easily negotiable with a buggy.

The cafe provides good value, simple food and the shop has a large variety of pocket money toys, as well as some more expensive but relevant treats like periscopes and rocket kits to tempt you.

All in all here is a place that thoroughly deserves its reputation as one of the top attractions in the Midlands. It's a brilliant day out for parents and kids of about 7 upwards – although not really designed for younger kids, there is so much going on that they are bound to enjoy the whole experience.

Fact File

● ADDRESS: Snibston Discovery Park, Ashby Road,Coalville, Leicestershire
● TELEPHONE: 01530 510 851 or 813 256
● DIRECTIONS: Follow the brown tourist signs from junction 22 of the M1 or junction 13 of M42
● PUBLIC TRANSPORT: No
● DISTANCE: 25 miles
● TRAVEL TIME: 35 minutes
● OPENING: 10.00am-5.00 pm daily
● PRICES: Adults £4.75, children £2.95, under 5s free. Colliery tour adults £1.00, children 50p
● RESTAURANT FACILITIES: Yes
● NAPPY CHANGING FACILITIES: Yes
● HIGH CHAIRS: Yes
● DOGS: No
● PUSHCHAIR-FRIENDLY: Yes
● NEARBY: Donington Grand Prix Motor Car Collection

National Birds of Prey Centre

"The Eagle has Landed . . ."

THIS IS ONE OF THOSE PLACES WHERE YOU'LL SEE SOMETHING that you thought you knew about from watching television or films and discover that there really is nothing like the real thing!

The first thing to bear in mind is that you need to time your visit so as not to miss the flying displays because these are what make the Birds of Prey Centre a unique and quite wonderful experience. Once you've felt the air move on your face as an owl swooshes past you and seen eagles fly, you know that any wildlife programme, however good, is still only television.

Because we'd cut it a bit fine we went straight to the flying field when we arrived – having visited the centre before, we knew that we'd get a lot more than just the impressive sight of magnificent birds in flight – the humans too put on a great show. John, in particular seems to be a born comic, as is Jemima Parry-Jones, the owner of the centre. The birds are flown every day; only heavy rain, strong winds or fog will keep them grounded. Some fly more energetically than others: the eagles have apparently learnt that they don't need to do much to get food so they do the bare minimum. And the American black vultures we saw flying are apparently much happier walking; though we were fortunate enough to be there to see all four take to the skies together for the first time – something the handlers

"You'll recognise the African white-backed vultures from *Jungle Book*"

had been working towards throughout the season. The four we saw were called Moet, Chandon, Dom and Perignon – each year the new birds born at the centre are named according to the year's chosen theme, and that year it was alcohol! With two of them on the lawn in front of the house and two on the flying field they flew back and forth, responding to calls (and food), gliding silently and hugely across the space in front of us. After the vultures, the lanner falcon came on. Although I've seen birds of prey hovering high above the fields where we live, I've never seen one 'stoop' – diving with folded wings at huge speed from a great height to catch their prey and it's a thrilling sight.

The highlight of a visit here may well be the flying itself but there's lots more to see: a hawk walk where the flying birds are tethered when they're not

in the air; the owl courtyard (there's something quite special about the look you get from an owl); and whatever you do, don't miss the huge aviaries housing birds with reputations as big as themselves – the African white-backed vultures (you'll recognise them from *Jungle Book*), golden eagles and, my favourite, the Andean condor. Until you've seen one of these it's impossible to believe a bird could be this size; the tail feathers look like oars for a small dinghy.

Before setting off for home and to prepare ourselves for the gift shop (just how little could we get away with today?) we were persuaded to stop off at the adventure play area for 10 minutes in exchange for a coffee-shop stop. There are lots of picnic benches nearby so you could spend a whole day here.

A final piece of advice is to buy the guide book, written by Jemima Parry-Jones: it's informative, nicely presented . . . and it made me laugh out loud.

Fact File

- ● ADDRESS: The National Birds of Prey Centre, Newent, Gloucestershire
- ● TELEPHONE: 01531 820286
- ● WEBSITE: www.nbpc.co.uk
- ● DIRECTIONS: M5 to junction 8, then M50 to junction3. Follow signs to Newent then brown tourist signs
- ● PUBLIC TRANSPORT: No
- ● DISTANCE: 60 miles
- ● TRAVEL TIME: 1 hour 30 minutes
- ● OPENING: Daily from February 1 to November 30, 10.30am-5.30pm (dusk if earlier)
- ● PRICES: £5.75 adults, £3.50 children, under-4's free, family ticket £16.50
- ● RESTAURANT FACILITIES: Yes
- ● NAPPY CHANGING FACILITIES: No
- ● HIGH CHAIRS: Yes
- ● DOGS: No
- ● PUSHCHAIR-FRIENDLY: Yes
- ● NEARBY: Three Choirs Vineyard (01531 890223)

National Sealife Centre

BUSTLING CENTRAL BIRMINGHAM DOES NOT, AT FIRST SIGHT, seem an obvious place to learn about fish, rivers, the sea and all other aspects of aquatic life. However, Birmingham's National Sea Life centre is big, bold and brilliant. Children are always fascinated by life underwater, and ours were no exception. From 18-months-old to adult, all of our group were kept enthralled by this excellent attraction. It is right in the city centre, overlooking one of the main canals, near the conference centre and the National Indoor Arena. We went by train, and it is an easy 10-minute buggy push from Snow Hill station.

The layout is an impressive spiral walkway, and as you walk in you are visually and aurally assaulted by the rushing torrents of water. Intermittent gushes of water in the very first tank take you

"The octopus provoked a morbid fascination with its agility and squidgy body"

completely by surprise! More than 55 different displays are designed to provide every habitat for what seemed an extraordinary range of fish and other sea and river creatures. The aquaria vary from ceiling height columns to wide shallow tanks. Shipwrecks and caves, rockpools and beaches with endless nooks and crannies provide realistic accommodation for the inhabitants. In the depths of the 'canal' lurked two enormous and scarily menacing pike, making the murky depths outside seem all the more sinister on the way home.

We were particularly taken with the charming seahorses: peering at them through convex magnifying portholes they seemed to peer back at us very intimately. All the fish looked shiny and well, even the great shoals of mackerel, circling their huge tank. The octopus provoked the most instant reaction – a morbid fascination with its agility and squidgy body, whilst the "best thing we saw" award went to, inevitably, the sharks. Some tanks let you poke your head up into a domed porthole, giving a new meaning to the phrase "eyeball to eyeball" confrontation.

We were amused by the apparently friendly dogfish which poked its nose up all along the ledge to talk to us. Shark and ray feeds are announced on the PA system, but otherwise ask at reception when you get there for any other feeding times (seahorses are particularly recommended).

At the top of the building is an atmospheric display about the sinking of the Titanic, followed by a rather spooky descent in a lift as if onto the wreck itself. It enthralled the children who enjoyed spotting unlikely deposits on the seabed, such as grand pianos, cases of champagne, and other luxury detritus of the sunk ship, as well as the menacingly roaming sharks and torpid rays which lurked all around.

Primary school aged children will enjoy following the Captain Pugwash quiz trail, answering questions on boards throughout the building. When we eventually emerged, blinking, into daylight and the gift

shop, the quiz-followers were given lollipops as prizes for completing their sheets, which went down well!

The cafe looked clean and pleasant, good-value, with a children's menu. We opted to eat away from the Centre on a nearby canal boat converted to a very narrow cafe. Situated in the refurbished and rebuilt Brindsleyplace area of the city, the Sea Life building is easily accessible on foot from the centre of town. It is a stunning part of the city and there is much to see in the immediate area. For our visit at the end of the Christmas holidays the whole area was wonderfully empty; possibly in the summer the canal towpaths would be less child friendly if they were more crowded. Take good strong straps for the newly-free-range toddler, or confine them to a buggy for the crucial parts of the walk. Conversely, energetic kids will love careering along the towpaths and the labyrinths of ramps and bridges along the canal sides, and the wide open spaces of the plaza are similarly appealing and wheel friendly.

Fact File

- ADDRESS: National Sealife Centre, The Waters Edge, Brindleyplace, Birmingham
- TELEPHONE: 0121 643 6777
- WEBSITE: www.sealife.co.uk
- DIRECTIONS: J6 off M6, follow signs to NIA. Park in NIA south car park. Sealife is just over the canal, and is well signed from NIA
- PUBLIC TRANSPORT: Train to Snow Hill and 10-minute walk. Follow signs for NIA
- DISTANCE: City centre
- TRAVEL TIME: 0
- OPENING: Daily from 10.00 am
- PRICES: Adults £8.00, children £5.50, family ticket £24.00
- RESTAURANT FACILITIES: Yes
- NAPPY CHANGING FACILITIES: Yes
- HIGH CHAIRS: Yes
- DOGS: No
- PUSHCHAIR-FRIENDLY: Yes
- NEARBY: Canals, waterways and towpaths of surrounding area

Royal Air Force Museum Cosford

One small step for mankind . . .

IF YOU ARE AT ALL INTO AEROPLANES, THEN THIS IS AN
excellent opportunity to see them at ground level
rather than as streaks in the sky. Here there are
three hangars packed full of aircraft representing
many eras of air travel and including warplanes,
transport, research and missile carrying aircraft.

As you drive in and park you'll be immediately
impressed by the huge aircraft parked casually
around. The museum is home to several ex-British
Airways planes which will tower over you as you
wander about. You can't get into many of them,
except on the Open Cockpit weekends (beginning of
the Spring and Autumn half term holidays), but
there are plenty of
viewing platforms so
you can get a good
look inside. On fine
days the Trident is
open to visitors,
though, and gave our
children their first
taste of being in an
aeroplane. They were amazed to see all the
switches and dials in the cockpit and the tiny galley
area – putting preparing tea for the family into a
wholly different perspective.

"Walk around and beneath the planes and marvel at the deeds they must have performed"

Walk up to the two hangars at the far end of the
airfield, where, in Hangar 2, you can see the
Research Collection. This has a number of unusual
and odd-looking aircraft: the first production Meteor,
the FD2 which broke the world airspeed record, and
an ejection seat demonstration. The new interactive
gallery is up here too, with a stimulating range of

flight-related displays and games – great for anyone over 5 (under-5's would be a bit daunted).

Move on through into Hangar 3, which houses the warplane collection. There are British, German, American and Japanese aircraft from the Second World War, and aircraft used in the Falklands and Gulf campaigns. Look out for the good guys – the Mosquito, Spitfire and Hurricane, as well as the enemy aeroplanes. You can walk around and beneath these beasts, play 'spot the baddy' with their identification logos, and generally marvel at the deeds they must have performed.

Back down at Hangar 1 is the transport and missile collection. Here you'll find a Polaris missile on display, broken up into five sections so you can see the individual rocket motors. You can also see the aero engine displays, and there is a

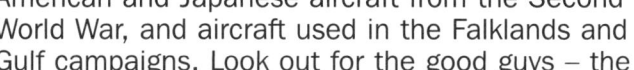

temporary exhibition gallery, photogallery and history of Cosford display too.

The Air Base is a 25-acre site in rural Shropshire. There are some large picnic sites and plenty of room to run about. Like all airfields though, it can get windy, so bring something to wrap up in if you need to. There is large restaurant and shop in the new Visitor centre.

Alongside the Air Base is usually a hive of air activity, which makes for interesting picnics. We watched small aircraft taking off and landing very close by. Each time we held our breath as they struggled airborne, and importantly busied off, only to be replaced by others arriving. There were also several gliders being pulled into the air and then circling back down to earth.

Watch out for the special events held at the Museum each year. The RAF Open Day is usually held on Father's Day (June) when the Base hosts many visiting aircraft, flown in for the occasion. It is a full 12 hours of entertainment and makes a great family day out, with flying displays as well as static aircraft to get close up to. There is also a Large Model Aircraft Rally held during July.

Fact File

- ADDRESS: RAF Museum, Cosford, Shifnal, Shropshire
- TELEPHONE: 01902 376200 or 0870 606 2027 (recorded)
- WEBSITE: www.rafmuseum.org.uk
- DIRECTIONS: 1 mile south from junction 3 of the M54, on the A41 in Wolverhampton direction
- PUBLIC TRANSPORT: None
- DISTANCE: 20 miles
- TRAVEL TIME: 45 minutes
- OPENING: 10.00am-6.00pm daily. Last admiccion 4.00pm
- PRICES: Adults £5.90, children free
- RESTAURANT FACILITIES: Yes
- NAPPY CHANGING FACILITIES: Yes, Ladies toilet
- HIGH CHAIRS: Yes
- DOGS: No
- PUSHCHAIR-FRIENDLY: Yes
- NEARBY: Telford or Weston Parks

The Shire Horse Centre

MORE THAN JUST A DAY LOOKING AT HORSES, A TRIP HERE gives you the chance to understand their daily lives, see some wonderful displays of animal skills and visit a Farm Park to boot! Not to mention Tractorland for young children, or the Hyperslide for everyone else and all in a lovely riverside setting.

There is a varied programme of events depending on the weather and how busy the Centre is. Most days during the summer you can start off with the Shire Horse Parade at about 11.00am, which is a good introduction to the animals. Be warned: they are not small! In fact, for the nervous, their sheer size and strength can be a bit daunting. With the whiff of straw and saddle leather in your nose, the jangle of bridles and the clatter of hooves on stone it is not difficult to imagine yourself a squire or a stable-lad in the days of yore, when these horses were as much a feature of daily life as the car is today. If there is no Parade you

> **"From the lofty heights of the wagon you get an unsurpassed view of all the animals kept in the paddocks"**

should be able to get a guided tour of the stables, but you can do your own tour of their living quarters regardless. You'll get a good, informative look at the daily routine of these huge beasts. We stroked a few noses but if your children are like ours and likely to be overwhelmed be prepared to do a fair amount of picking up and cajoling inside the stables.

They will undoubtedly enjoy the next bit though – a wagon ride around the Centre, available most days. You travel in style, being pulled along behind

the enormous brown haunches of Jacob, and from
the lofty heights of the wagon get an unsurpassed
view of all the animals kept in the paddocks. The
ride lasts about 10 minutes and is accompanied by
a commentary. Indoors again, climb aboard a
motorised car for a video and ride through the
Country Village experience, which gives a good
insight into country life in the 1920's.

Rides over, we clambered down and re-did the
wagon route on foot, which gave us the chance to
see everything at ground level. There are goats,
lambs, foals, calves, pigs and chickens all to meet,
and plenty of opportunity to get in and touch them.
All the paths are easily accessible with a pushchair.

Next to the Arena are the play areas. These are
very good, with something for all ages. Tractorland
was a great hit with our boys. It's a mini figure of
eight circuit with any number of pedal tractors of all

sizes, and kept them amused for ages. Alongside, for those of us too big to ride on pedal tractors, is the Hyperslide complex – a fantastically coloured and contorted series of slides, just great for letting your hair down on.

With other sorts of play equipment around – trampolines, real tractors to scramble on, sand pit and indoor playbarn – there is plenty to distract the children. When (if!) they tire of all this activity persuade them to visit the demonstration barn, where during the morning and afternoon Pat-A-Pet sessions they can hold rabbits, guinea pigs and various other pet animals.

Events vary during the year, and as 2001 is the Centre's 10th anniversary there are lots of extra events planned. Check in advance for details of what is going on.

Fact File

- ADDRESS: The Shire Horse Centre, Clifford Road, Stratford-on-Avon, Warwickshire
- TELEPHONE: 01789 266276/415274 (answerphone)
- DIRECTIONS: M40 to junction 15, then A46 and A439 to Stratford (Town Centre). Follow signs to Broadway, and then to Shire Horse Centre. 1 mile south of town
- PUBLIC TRANSPORT: No
- DISTANCE: 30 miles
- TRAVEL TIME: 50 minutes
- OPENING: 10.00am-5.00pm daily all year, except November to February when it is closed Thursdays and Fridays. Closed in January. No weekday wagon rides during the winter
- PRICES: Adults £5.50, children £4.50, under-2's free (except in playbarn). Reduced prices in winter
- RESTAURANT FACILITIES: Yes
- NAPPY CHANGING FACILITIES: Yes
- HIGH CHAIRS: Yes
- DOGS: Yes
- PUSHCHAIR-FRIENDLY: Yes
- NEARBY: Stratford-on-Avon Butterfly Farm (01789 299288)

The Great Outdoors

Coombe Country Park

IT IS EASY TO IMAGINE YOURSELVES PART OF A JANE AUSTEN novel as you drive up Coombe Abbey's long, tree-lined drive. The drive is just a taste of what's to come, with the park itself offering woodland and lakeside walks, beautiful gardens, and an abundance of wildlife. It has a network of all-weather pathways, fortunately for us, as the heavens opened as we arrived.

"There are special stages at the water's edge where you can scoop up a jam jar of weed and pond-life"

Our first port of call was to the Visitor Centre, to shelter from the rain. This includes a Discovery Centre, as well as restaurant, shop and toilet facilities. The Discovery Centre is well worth visiting as it tells you all about the wildlife of the park and gives seasonal information. It has some great interactive games for children to play. They pressed buttons and watched lights come on, showing them where the woodpeckers and the squirrels live. They put their hands in covered boxes and felt different kinds of tree bark. And they sniffed at different smells in scent boxes, and watched tiny fish swimming around in a mock pond. The Centre also sells or hires some essential kit for the day: nature detective kits, pond dipping equipment and mini-beast collecting pots. Guided walks with rangers start here too, with a varying programme of topical and seasonal themes on offer (some with a small charge and bookable in advance).

Once the rain eased off sufficiently we ventured out. It was too wet for the adjoining playground, so we began our walk through the park. We walked and we walked and we walked. The rain made it all seem like more of an adventure, and of course the puddles were great for splashing in!

We started with the Formal Gardens and Arboretum, by following the path down towards the lake, and what a lake! It stretches as far as you can see, and its ducks are well-used to humans. As we approached they came swimming up, looking for the bread which we had forgotten to bring. Be careful with children around the lake as there is no fencing.

Leaving the ducks behind, we continued through the Arboretum, marvelling at the size of the redwood trees growing on a small slope up from the path. In drier times this would a great place for hide and seek behind the enormous tree trunks: we had to give up because the slope proved too slippery for small legs to cope with. So, trousers muddied, we carried on. Wrautum, whoever he (?) was, certainly had a big field. This is the ideal place for kicking a ball, flying a kite or just having a good run round, rain or no rain. There is an adventure playground here too, with bridges to cross and ladders to climb.

The wander round the Duck Decoy Spinney next was our favourite. Here the trees grow so closely together the rain could hardly get through so we were able to pull our hoods down and free our ears. The path running around pools and amongst dense undergrowth was, nevertheless, very pushchair-friendly. There are lots of different trees, and interpretation boards along the way illustrating the animals and birds that live there. Even if you don't see any animals, the boards provide a talking point for children, and we chatted our way round wondering where the animals and birds were hiding. The woods have a magical feel: we imagined fairies and gnomes watching us as we walked through. For pond dippers there are special stages at the water's edge where you can scoop up a jam jar of weed and pond-life, but here again you must be careful that little ones don't take a tumble.

If you plan to picnic here, you'll find benches in abundance and lots of grass for spreading out your rug. For the more adventurous there is a barbecue area next to the car park, where there are barbecues next to picnic tables; all you have to do is bring your own charcoal and food and enjoy an open air feast.

Fact File

● ADDRESS: Coombe Country Park, Brinklow Road, Binley, Coventry, West Midlands
● TELEPHONE: 01203 453720
● DIRECTIONS: M6 to junction 2 and follow signs
● PUBLIC TRANSPORT: Bus 913 from Coventry city centre
● DISTANCE: 20 miles
● TRAVEL TIME: 40 minutes
● OPENING: Daily 7.30am-dusk. Visitor Centre 9.30am-6.00pm (summer) and 9.30am-4.00pm (winter)
● PRICES: Parking from £1.00 (1 hour) to £3.00 (all day)
● RESTAURANT FACILITIES: Yes
● NAPPY CHANGING FACILITIES: Yes
● HIGH CHAIRS: Yes
● DOGS: Yes
● PUSHCHAIR-FRIENDLY: Yes
● NEARBY: Midland Air Museum at Coventry Airport (01203 301033), Museum of British Road Transport in Coventry (01203 832425)

Dudmaston

Five, six, pick up sticks

IDEAL FOR A SUNDAY AFTERNOON, THE EXTENSIVE LAKESIDE gardens and farmland of Dudmaston's 17th century house always make a welcome trip out in our family, holding a fascination for the children of which they never tire. Dudmaston is popular with all ages but there is plenty of room and you will always be able to find a secluded spot.

The estate is situated on the banks of the river Severn in Quatt near Bridgnorth, and as you drive through the gates you cross large sheep grazing areas which will be full of bouncy lambs in the early Spring. Even the parking area is picturesque, situated in an old walled garden of the house, and today still a beautiful orchard of apple and pear trees. Although you can visit the house with its fine furniture, sculptures and flower paintings, the main attraction for those with children is the grounds and so usually we spend our afternoon exploring.

> **"Walk across the fields, climb trees, clamber over stiles and generally do all the things associated with a day in the countryside"**

Entry to the grounds is through a small door in the wall and as soon as you step through it's as if you have stepped back in years and entered a secret garden. The gardens drop down to a large lake, and the lawned slopes make excellent rolling areas for children: always a hit with our brood. There are plenty of places to sit and watch children play or you can roam through rockeries on a voyage of discovery. Of many memorable visits, one Spring day stands out, when we pitched ourselves beneath the magnolia trees, and got covered in marvellously-scented petals which snowed down every time the wind blew.

You can leave the garden area and walk across farmland and woodland areas either to the lake or on to the Dingle, a wetted woodland valley, which is very secluded and unspoiled. A leaflet showing both walks can be bought for £1.00. Swans live on the lake and they sometimes nest very close to the shore, so you can sit and watch their comings and goings.

The real treat here though is being able to walk across the fields, climb trees, clamber over stiles and generally do all the things associated with a day in the countryside, and in a totally unspoiled setting. We always return from our visits laden with grasses, leaves, sticks, acorns, bits of sheep's wool pulled off a fence, feathers, anything the children find; the usual treasure trove from a day out in the country. Ending up on the walls at home, or pulled out of a less-used pocket, we have an ongoing reminder of our visit!

Back at the car park there is a small snack bar offering a tempting array of home made cakes and pastries. As it is open before the rest of the estate you can get something to eat before you go in.

Fact File

- ADDRESS: Dudmaston, Quatt, Bridgnorth, Shropshire
- TELEPHONE: 01746 780866
- WEBSITE: www.nationaltrust.org.uk
- DIRECTIONS: 4 miles south east of Bridgnorth on the A442
- PUBLIC TRANSPORT: Bus route Midland Red 297 Kidderminster to Bridgnorth
- DISTANCE: 40 miles
- TRAVEL TIME: 1 hour
- OPENING: Sunday to Wednesday 12.00noon-6.00pm from beginning April to end September. House 2.00pm-6.00pm and closed Mondays
- PRICES: Garden £2.80 adults, £1.30 children. House and garden £3.85 adults, £2.30 children, under-5's free. Family £9.00. Free to National Trust members
- RESTAURANT FACILITIES: Yes
- NAPPY CHANGING FACILITIES: Yes
- HIGH CHAIRS: Yes
- DOGS: Grounds only
- PUSHCHAIR-FRIENDLY: Yes
- NEARBY: Childhood & Costume Museum in Bridgnorth (01746 768550)

Hawkstone Park

SEIZE YOUR TORCHES AND DON THOSE STOUT WALKING SHOES! Lances, shields and swords will not actually be required although you may well fancy bringing them to indulge in a spot of dragon-slaying whilst you are here. A feast for the imagination, a visit to Hawkstone Park is a bit like setting out on a Famous Five adventure: great for knights and castles devotees, but not recommended for those with pushchairs or youngsters unable to walk very far.

The Park consists of a heavily wooded valley between steep rock outcrops. Follies, castles and labyrinth were created within it over a hundred years ago, but fell into disuse. Recently it has been restored and re-opened as a sort of historic theme park – only the rides are ones you scramble up yourselves and the features are natural rock formations. Make sure you are all feeling energetic before you attempt it and do heed signposts and safety information.

At the entrance we found the shop, toilets (use these as it is a long walk to the only others) and information area with a 5-minute safety video for those with children. Torches can be bought here for £2.00 and you can hire child carriers too. Then we faced our first dilemma of the day. Was it to be the full historic walk (about 3 hours) or were we to

"Secret valleys, caves, towers and follies to be mastered just like in a good old Dungeons and Dragons game"

opt for one of the two shorter walks (one or two hours)? Never willing to turn down a challenge we decided we wanted to explore all there was and set off at a good pace along the signposted green route with the children having great fun with the torches

and fighting imaginary sword fights at every tree.

You will soon realise why there are so many warning signs, as there really is something unexpected at every turn. The path winds and twists through the landscape, narrow in places, widening out in others and plunging up and down through cliffs, rock faces and tunnels. Up the 152 steps (not for the faint-hearted or very young) to the Monument Tower you can survey 12 counties on a good day, before descending once more to whatever fantasy you choose. There are clefts in the rocks, enclosed passageways, secret valleys, caves, towers and follies to be mastered just like in a good old Dungeons and Dragons game. In some caves you will need torches as they are unlit for short distances, providing great opportunities for scary noises and general mayhem.

Impossible to list all the surprises, suffice to say that the children loved it, though favourites were the rustic bridges, clefts and grottoes. Grotto Hill, with its underground labyrinth and viewing area is pretty spooky but makes an ideal 'treasure cave' to head for, whilst on your way back you will pass Foxes' Knob and Reynard's Walk, and meet King Arthur.

There are several places to picnic along the route and an excellent tea room back at the entrance. Repose here whilst you assess the Sorcerers you've disposed of and gloat over your treasure!

Fact File

● ADDRESS: Hawkstone Park & Follies, Weston-under-Redcastle, Shrewsbury, Shropshire
● TELEPHONE: 01939 200611
● WEBSITE: www.hawkstone.co.uk
● DIRECTIONS: Located between Shrewsbury and Whitchurch just off the A49. Use M54 and junction 6 exit towards Whitchurch on the A442. Beyond Hodnet follow signs to Weston-under-Redcastle and Hawkstone
● PUBLIC TRANSPORT: None
● DISTANCE: 50 miles
● TRAVEL TIME: 1 hour 15 minutes
● OPENING: Wednesday-Sunday from 31 March to 28 October 10.30am-dusk, daily in July and August. Weekends only January to March
● PRICES: Adults £4.50, children £2.50, family £12.00. 50p extra per person at weekends. Reduced price winter weekends
● RESTAURANT FACILITIES: Yes
● NAPPY CHANGING FACILITIES: Yes
● HIGH CHAIRS: Yes
● DOGS: Yes
● PUSHCHAIR-FRIENDLY: No
● NEARBY: Shrewsbury town, with its Tudor buildings, Abbey and Castle

Kenilworth Castle

Some days the kids just can't cope with being careful, walking not running, not touching everything; they just want fresh air, space and something to explore. Kenilworth Castle is just the place: the largest castle ruin in England, giving children ample scope to imagine the magnificent lives led by people in medieval England, as well as rushing up and down stairs, in and out of tunnels and passages and tumbling on the grass.

The castle is enormous. It comes on you totally unexpectedly. "Wow", there it is, tall and splendid, the massive red sandstone building glowing over the countryside, magnificent and atmospheric. Roam at will over the ruins first, but leave time to charge about the numerous walks in the grounds too (free if you don't enter the castle).

Open to the sky now, the Norman-built keep provides an endless variety of places to explore, peer at and

"A path skirts all around the outside edge of the Castle walls giving a looming view of the buildings from every angle"

clamber in and out of. There is a fascinating amount of detail still visible here, and the children loved the huge fireplaces which are now perched high on the walls. There are brilliant spiral staircases, secret passages leading into cul de sacs, and suitably dank and horrible cellar type rooms. Nothing is very intimidating or difficult, but a toddler wouldn't want to be too far from Mum or Dad. Some upper floors are intact and have lovely wide windows looking out over the Warwickshire countryside. From there it's the matter of a daydream to imagine the pointed hats, veils, sweeping gowns and robes of the Middle Ages.

Outside the walls the Tudor gardens are laid out in complex patterns of hip-high clipped box hedges – a giant knot garden – irresistible for kids to rush in and out of the sections, hiding behind the dumpy yew trees and racing up and down the length of the gardens. For a peace and quiet try the knot garden by the North entrance with its clipped lavenders and rosemary.

Even the car park is fun, a flat grassy area, surrounded by what appear to be massive earthworks left from a previous incarnation, which are topped by huge beech trees. Behind is a giant ditch, great for a quick game of cowboys and Indians, even without going into the castle itself!

For the energetic family whose children haven't run and climbed themselves into a heap by now, there are other walks and areas to explore. A path skirts all around the outside edge of the Castle walls giving a looming view of the buildings from every angle. A robust buggy would cope on this path, but there are some steps along the way.

Further afield the Millennium Trail takes you on a 1-mile circular walk out to the remains of the enormous pleasure house built for Henry V. Buggy pushers can go along the lane, if they'd prefer, rather

than taking to the fields and hedges. There are no steep hills though, so with suitable refreshments and guile, short legs could manage it.

Visitors here are well-catered for with free information leaflets and children's activity sheets, as well as audio tours for adults and children, also free of charge. In the restored stable there is an interactive model of the castle and its grounds, showing how it has developed over the centuries. The shop has a well-chosen selection of stock, whilst the simple tea rooms are in the same building. They provide much needed refreshments, but not a full meal. Inside the castle walls, there is a large area of grass for your picnic with tall trees, and the walls themselves for shade if needed.

Returning from the Castle on the left towards the town is Abbey Fields, a huge green space with lake, ducks, play area and ample room for football and picnics. There is also a nice open air swimming pool in Kenilworth.

Fact File

- ADDRESS: Kenilworth Castle, Kenilworth, Warwickshire
- TELEPHONE: 01926 852078
- WEBSITE: www.english-heritage.org.uk
- DIRECTIONS: A45 and A452 to Kenilworth. Clearly signposted from town centre
- PUBLIC TRANSPORT: Stagecoach Midland Red X18 bus between Coventry and Stratford calls at the castle (01926 414140). 5 miles from Warwick train station
- DISTANCE: 25 miles
- TRAVEL TIME: 30-45 minutes
- OPENING: Daily 10.00am-4.00pm
- PRICES: Adults £4.00, children £2.00, under-5's and English Heritage members free
- RESTAURANT FACILITIES: Yes (tea room)
- NAPPY CHANGING FACILITIES: Yes
- HIGH CHAIRS: Yes
- DOGS: On leads
- PUSHCHAIR-FRIENDLY: Yes
- NEARBY: Abbey Fields, Warwick Castle

Ragley Hall

Definitely a stately home plus, with all there is to do here you'll find yourself running out of time! There's a tremendous adventure wood, a maze, formal gardens, stables, and 400-acres of glorious letting-off steam parkland to explore, all complimented by a relaxed and friendly family atmosphere throughout.

We like to start off in the aptly named Adventure Wood because that's where the maze is. It is a fantastic design, operating on two levels with paved pathways, rope bridges, tunnels and other constructions. Avoid the upper level with small children or pushchairs as it really is too difficult, but even on the lower level we guarantee you'll get lost anyway! (Make sure no one needs the loo before you go in: we didn't and our hunt for the exit became increasingly desperate!) Once in the centre of the

"The Woodland Walk is an enjoyable stroll with trees, plants and wildlife"

maze you'll find a small play area with slides, and thankfully, an easy exit to the rest of the delights of the Adventure Wood. Although essentially a large adventure playground it is well-designed in two sections for over-12's and under-12's with all the swings, climbing frames and wobbly walkways that kids enjoy after a car ride. It is a no-dog zone.

Nearby is a vast picnic area next to the lake, with

plenty of tables and loads of room to run around or kick a ball. Bring your own food here or try Bodger's Cabin on the edge of the picnic area. As well as food and drinks this sells frisbees, bats, and balls in case you've forgotten to bring them – a thoughtful touch.

You can walk up to the Hall either through the parkland or through the gardens. Those with pushchairs may find the gravel paths rather hard work, in which case it is best to follow the road up. The gardens are well worth seeing, as they have been laid out with lawns and trees. And then behind the trees the house itself rises up, dwarfing everyone with its huge columns adorning the front entrance, and steep steps up.Inside the house are some splendid portraits and treasures, not greatly appreciated by our young children although they were fascinated by some pictures and kept asking if the people depicted were still alive. For older children there is a good pamphlet guide with questions and explanations to point out more eccentric items which appeal to children. Pushchairs are allowed in the Hall, which is a welcome concession, but there are quite a few steps.

Back outside again, seek out the stables and carriage collection. The family horses are kept there so there are a few noses to stroke. We enjoyed looking at all the carriages. Nearby is an exhibition of Edwardian dolls and toys, behind glass unfortunately, but included in the garden entrance price and worth a quick look as the children will enjoy seeing familiar, but oh-so-different, toys.

As you leave the stables you should just have time to do the Woodland Walk, which is an enjoyable stroll with trees, plants and wildlife to see. It is about two miles long and often very peaceful, though not recommended with a pushchair. Don't miss the ice-house and venison house – both are suitably dark and gloomy to peer in!

Fact File

- ADDRESS: Ragley Hall, Alcester, Warwickshire
- TELEPHONE: 01789 762090
- DIRECTIONS: A435 from Birmingham or from M42 junction 3. 2 miles south west of Alcester. Signposted
- PUBLIC TRANSPORT: Midland Red bus 146 from Birmingham Bull Ring. Hourly service, does not run Sundays (0121 200 2700)
- DISTANCE: 20 miles
- TRAVEL TIME: 35 minutes
- OPENING: Gardens 10.00am-6.00pm from 9 April to end September, Thursday to Sunday and BH Mondays. Daily in Easter, May half term and summer school holidays
- PRICES: Gardens adults £4.50, children £3.50, under-5's free, family £15.00. Extra for House
- RESTAURANT FACILITIES: Yes
- NAPPY CHANGING FACILITIES: Yes
- HIGH CHAIRS: Yes
- DOGS: Limited areas
- PUSHCHAIR-FRIENDLY: Yes
- NEARBY: Golden Cross Inn, Ardens Grafton, near Bidford-on-Avon (01789 772420) is a family pub with antique doll and teddy bear collection

Somewhat Historical

Acton Scott Historic Working Farm

Step back, and re-live life on an upland farm at the turn of the century. Acton Scott is an open working farm in the Shropshire hills, with a difference. Its aim is to let you experience the old ways of farming in a safe environment. The authenticity of the farm has been maintained, so don't expect many of the commercial trappings of the 1990's.

We were met at the gate by sheep who were very eager to escort us and ready to share our lunch. Wonderfully tame, they provided a super welcome. There are plenty of picnic tables set up all around the farm.

On different days there are demonstrations of butter making, bread baking and hand milking, plus visits to the farm by a blacksmith, a farrier and a

"Look out for lambing, shearing, cider making or steam threshing"

wheelwright. There is also a programme of events during holidays and half terms which follows the farming year. Look out for lambing, shearing, cider making or steam threshing at the appropriate times of the year. Special demonstrations, held mainly at the weekends, demonstrate more of the tasks that would have been going on: brick making, basket making, spinning, smocking, making corn dollies and besom brooms to name just a few. When we went we had a good chat with the beekeeper, the children looking into the hives to see the honeycomb and finding out about different types of honey.

For younger children, possibly distracted during a detailed demonstration, there is a playhouse in the outbuildings where the demonstrations take place. But for everyone, the living willow maze makes a great play area. It is in a cartwheel shape and has gates, stiles, tunnels and hurdles.

As well as being a working farm Acton Scott is also a museum of farm machinery which is safely scattered around. Most is well-labelled and easily viewed by children. There is a waggoner with a team of Shire horses continually at work, so throughout the day horses are harnessed into different farm

machinery. We watched a horse powering a mill to grind corn and really helping to bring history to life.

Ducks, chickens and sheep roam freely and you can expect to find them anywhere, especially in the shade under your car on a hot day. There is a patient donkey who won our hearts and had to be revisited several times. The cobbled main farmyard comes straight from a children's picture book and has everything children would expect to find, even the smelly manure heap!

Do follow the walk across the fields – surprisingly few people do. It's a circular nature trail and worth attempting even with a young child. We came across an old shepherd's caravan complete with shepherd. The going is a bit rough for a pushchair, and it may be a good idea to bring a backpack for the baby. Don't forget wellies either if it has been at all wet.

There is a cafe on the farm which is situated in the old schoolhouse. It is a most idyllic setting and they serve a good range of hot and cold snacks including homemade cakes.

Fact File

● ADDRESS: Acton Scott Historic Working Farm, Wenlock Lodge, Acton Scott, near Church Stretton, Shropshire
● TELEPHONE: 01694 781306/7
● WEBSITE: www.actonscottmuseum.co.uk
● DIRECTIONS: M54, then A5 to Shrewsbury. Pick up the A49 south towards Ludlow, and it is signposted off the A49 just beyond Church Stretton
● PUBLIC TRANSPORT: None
● DISTANCE: 60 miles
● TRAVEL TIME: 1 hour 30 minutes
● OPENING: 10.00am-5.00pm Tuesday to Sunday and Bank Holidays, 3 April to 28 October
● PRICES: Adults £3.95, children £1.50, under-5's free, family £11.50
● RESTAURANT FACILITIES: Yes
● NAPPY CHANGING FACILITIES: Yes
● HIGH CHAIRS: Yes
● DOGS: No
● PUSHCHAIR-FRIENDLY: No
● NEARBY: Carding Mill Valley and Long Mynd for excellent walks

Avoncroft Museum of Historic Buildings

And a small cabin build there,
of clay and wattles made

DON'T BE DETERRED BY THE NAME: AVONCROFT IS A
fascinating place for families with children of all
ages. Sited in an extensive grassy area with plenty
of trees, it's an open-air museum light years away
from fusty collections of fossils. Children can run
and scramble with no fear of damaging themselves
or the exhibits, whilst for older people it offers an
incomparable opportunity to step back in time.

The Museum's objective is to rescue buildings
from destruction. It has over 20 buildings re-erected
which have been collected from all over the Heart of
England and from a host of different uses. Ranging
from a 14th century
beamed roof to a
1940's pre-fab
(complete with period
furnishings) together
they span 600 years
of British history. Each
building provides a
snap-shot of its
particular period's life
in Britain so as you walk into each one you really
feel the atmosphere of bygone days. Get a
guidebook as you start out as this gives a map of
the site and a suggested route as well as
information on the source and history of each
building.

Every exhibit has something special to offer, from
the sleeping prisoner we saw through the spy-hole
of his cell door to the welcoming fire in the 15th
century Merchant's House. It's all authentically

**"Excellent guides are
on hand in many
buildings to give
insights into the
previous inhabitants"**

done, and attention to detail is superb. Excellent guides are on hand in many buildings to give insights into the previous inhabitants – we especially liked the story of the family of eleven who lived in the tiny Toll House in the 19th century. Some buildings are still used, such as the green tin-roofed Mission Chapel, complete with working organ, where services are held by a local vicar.

Recent additions to the collection include an old-style police box – familiar to all of us generations of Dr Who watchers – and village church spire you can

peer up inside. But our favourite building is the Windmill. Built in the 19th century it is a classic child's round brick and clapboard mill. You can go inside and climb up into the milling section where stoneground wholemeal flour is produced (on sale at the shop).

There are usually special activities going on at the Museum, with regular demonstrations of a blacksmith at work, woodturning, chainmaking, racksawing and brickmaking. There are also farm animals around the site and on some weekends a miniature track railway is open for rides. There is a large picnic area with plenty of tables.

We visited midweek during the school holidays when it was very peaceful. However it is often busy with school trips during the summer term.

Fact File

- ADDRESS: Avoncroft Museum of Historic Buildings, Stoke Heath, Bromsgrove, Worcestershire
- TELEPHONE: 01527 831886
- WEBSITE: www.avoncroft.org.uk
- DIRECTIONS: Just off the A38, 2 miles south of Bromsgrove. M42 junction 1, or between M5 junctions 4 and 5
- PUBLIC TRANSPORT: 2 miles from Bromsgrove station. Trains from Birmingham and Worcester (0121 643 2711)
- DISTANCE: 20 miles
- TRAVEL TIME: 45 minutes
- OPENING: Beginning March to end November 10.30am-5.00pm (to 5.30pm at weekends and dusk in winter). Daily in July and August; closed Fridays in other months
- PRICES: Adults £5.00, children £2.50, family £13.50, under-5's free
- RESTAURANT FACILITIES: Yes
- NAPPY CHANGING FACILITIES: Yes
- HIGH CHAIRS: No
- DOGS: Yes
- PUSHCHAIR-FRIENDLY: Yes
- NEARBY: Forge Mill Needle Museum (01527 62509) a museum and parkland, or Hanbury Hall (01527 821214) house and gardens

The Black Country Living Museum

ALTHOUGH AN INDUSTRIAL HERITAGE MUSEUM MAY NOT SOUND a winner for children, be assured, a trip here makes an excellent day out, with something for everyone. Based on a 26-acre site in the heart of the Black Country, this museum is a living tribute to how people lived and worked in the region after the Industrial Revolution. It is a large site, so to really do it justice you will need to spend a whole day here or to return on several occasions. Take a pushchair if you have young children who cannot walk very far.

The whole site is accessible to pushchairs although the cobbled streets may prove quite difficult at times and you have to park pushchairs outside some buildings. This museum is always very busy and is especially popular with school groups so it is advisable to arrive early.

On arrival we made straight for the Village, travelling there in style by tram. Faithfully-restored houses, factories and shops are to be found here. Each of the buildings is staffed by people from the Black Country wearing period dress

"We were invited to podge some new rugs, blacklead the grates and renew the newspaper doilies"

and you'll find them working on the crafts or activities they would have done at the time. They were brilliant with the children and indeed one lady offered our children a week's holiday to podge some new rugs, blacklead the grates and renew the newspaper doilies in the cupboards. Needless to say there were no takers and the children beat a hasty retreat down the garden only to find a rather primitive double privy!

Most popular was the "Suck Shop" where we stocked up for the day, having been assured that the sweets had not been flavoured and coloured with mercury and arsenic as they once were. The bakery was another hit with the children (we didn't need our picnics after the Lardy cakes), whereas at the school we escaped unscathed from the Victorian lesson whose strict teacher threatened one of the class with the cane for having "scrumped the vicar's apples".

Around the Village there is a network of canals. You'll need to watch toddlers in this area, but the 45-minute narrow boat rides are an added attraction in the summer (£2.90 adults and £2.50 children). Our four-year-olds loved it, especially the tunnel, but be warned that all the lights are switched off at some stages. A bit further on is the Mine, included in the entrance price. You can go down along to the coal face and pit bottom with a guide, but although there are no age restrictions, it is very dark, authentic and claustrophobic, and probably not for youngsters.

Don't miss the old fairground though. All the old fashioned rides are there including favourites such as the swing boats, helter skelter and the cake walk. The rides cost extra (between 50p and £1.00 each).

For lunch you can't really beat good old fish and chips wrapped in paper from the fried fish shop in the Village, although there is a cafe in the Stables block nearby too. Also there are plenty of picnic tables around, and large running around areas for children if they still have any energy left.

Fact File

- ADDRESS: Black Country Living Museum, Tipton Road, Dudley, W. Midlands
- TELEPHONE: 0121 557 9643
- WEBSITE: www.bclm.co.uk
- DIRECTIONS: Off the A4123, three miles from M5 junction 2. Signposted
- PUBLIC TRANSPORT: Train to Tipton station from Birmingham. Short bus ride from opposite station. Buses direct from Dudley to Museum
- DISTANCE: 5 miles
- TRAVEL TIME: 15 minutes
- OPENING: 10.00am-5.00pm daily March to October. 10.00am-4.00pm Wednesday to Sunday from November to February
- PRICES: Adult £7.95, child £4.75, family £21.50. Under-5's free
- RESTAURANT FACILITIES: Yes
- NAPPY CHANGING FACILITIES: Yes
- HIGH CHAIRS: Yes
- DOGS: No
- PUSHCHAIR-FRIENDLY: Yes
- NEARBY: Dudley Canal Trust Trips underneath Dudley Castle hill (01384 236275)

Blists Hill Victorian Town

IF YOUR IDEA OF MUSEUMS IS OF QUIET REVERENT PLACES where you spend your time reading notices, then be prepared for something different here. Blists Hill is in the open air for a start, and it vividly re-creates our industrial heritage using characters from Victorian England. Located in the birthplace of the Industrial Revolution, it has relocated many original buildings of the period and has few written explanations. The result is a real change from a traditional museum and a fascinating day out.

The museum is a 50-acre site with a series of buildings, some original, some moved from other sites and some reconstructions, reflecting town life at the turn of the century: the bank, the doctor, the school, the grocer and baker, and, most memorably, the Iron Works. Inside the buildings people dressed in period costume explain and demonstrate what they would have been doing there at the time.

"You can see red hot molten iron being poured into ladles and moulds"

Make sure you don't miss the Bank! It's the first building you come to and is essential, because here you change your 20th century money for token pennies, halfpennies and farthings of the time. You'll need this old money to buy any products of the demonstrations: from freshly-baked bread and sweets, butcher's pies and beer, to candles and wrought iron goods.

Bbuy a guide to the buildings to make sure that you don't miss anything out. There is loads to see and a tremendous amount going on, such as the Fairground with its Victorian roundabout and swingboats. During the school holidays you'll find several extras; Punch and Judy shows and donkey rides. At other times of the year look out for Steam Weekends and a "Ladies Day" in May.

Our favourites included the pigsties, and the candlemaker's workshop. Here you can watch the whole process from winding the wicks to dipping the candles and hanging them out to dry. With all of those candles hanging from the ceiling, our 2-year-old burst into a chorus of "Happy Birthday to you"!

The working foundry pours hot metal every Wednesday, when you can see red hot molten iron being poured into ladles and moulds to make all

kinds of cast iron products, including Punch and Judy doorstops. It is a spectacular sight.

Blists Hill is great with a pushchair, as everywhere has ramped access and the paths between the buildings are well laid-out. If it's crowded in a particular building you may find it difficult to take a pushchair in, but it seemed safe to leave them outside. If you need a rest, horse and trap rides around the site are on offer.

For a change from the buildings you can do a very pleasant walk along the towpath of the Shropshire Canal. You can picnic along here, or there is also a large grassy area near the Fairground, but take something to sit on as there are not many picnic tables. There are several places where you can buy food too, including the reconstructed Forest Green pavilion.

Fact File

● ADDRESS: Blists Hill Victorian Town, near Ironbridge, Shropshire
● TELEPHONE: 01952 433522/432166
● WEBSITE: www.ironbridge.org.uk
● DIRECTIONS: M6 to M54, leave at junction 4, follow signs to Ironbridge Gorge Museum, and then signs for Blists Hill Open Air Museum
● PUBLIC TRANSPORT: Train to Telford Central Station and 6 miles taxi/bus ride to Madeley. Or X96 bus from Birmingham to Madeley, and 15-minute walk to Museum (0345 056785)
● DISTANCE: 40 miles
● TRAVEL TIME: 1 hour
● OPENING: Daily 1st April to 5 November 10.00am-5.00pm, and Saturday-Wednesday 10.00am-4.00pm the rest of the year
● PRICES: Adults £7.50, children £5.00, under-5's free
● RESTAURANT FACILITIES: Yes
● NAPPY CHANGING FACILITIES: Yes
● HIGH CHAIRS: Yes
● DOGS: Yes
● PUSHCHAIR-FRIENDLY: Yes
● NEARBY: The other 8 Ironbridge Gorge Museums, including the Teddy Bear Shop near the Ironbridge Visitor Centre, and the chance to don a hard hat and go underground at the Tar Tunnel. Passport tickets to all sites available

Boscobel House & Moseley Old Hall

<small>Follow in the footsteps of Charles</small> II <small>by visiting</small> Boscobel and Moseley. Charles fled from the Roundheads at the Battle of Worcester in 1651, and was hidden in various places in the Heart of England until he could escape to France. His most famous hiding place is undoubtedly Boscobel House, then an isolated hunting lodge. Now owned by English Heritage, it is an excellent way to introduce children to historical events: a story well within their grasp, a small house to tour, plenty of space outside to run around, and the chance to inspect the famous 'Royal Oak'.

"There are references all around the house to the visit of the Prince"

You need to visit the house with a guided tour, which takes about 30 minutes. These do not need to be booked. Our guide did a grand job of bringing the story to life for the children. The house still has many original features which would have been there when Prince Charles came, in particular the priest holes, used to hide Catholics and, once, a fugitive future King.

One brave member of the group volunteered to try out a priest hole for size. It was situated in the closet, and the children were amazed to hear that a thunderbox toilet would have been placed over the entrance as the smell would put any dogs searching the house off the scent!

The actual priest hole used to conceal Prince Charles is in the attic and very small. It didn't have a toilet over the entrance, but instead the cheese was stored over it to provide alternative scents for dogs searching with the Parliamentary troops. Today,

there are references all around the house to the visit of the Prince, and we had fun guessing which door he might have entered by (we know only that it was at the back). Once you've finished in the house, make sure you wander in the gardens. Charles apparently hid for the best part of a day in an oak tree in the grounds before reaching the house itself. A descendant of that tree still stands proudly nearby, a mere 300 years-old. You can walk out across the field to it, and we collected acorns from the "King's Tree", and peered up into the branches.

In the rest of the grounds there are some outhouses containing historical farm machinery, a Victorian Dairy and a 17th century barn; plenty to entertain young children. There is also a tea garden and large picnic area.

From Boscobel Charles escaped to Moseley Old Hall, about 10 miles away, so, if the kids are still interested, follow his trail there. It's a small Elizabethan house with amazing old sloping floors. To children it must seem like the crooked house they read about. Like Boscobel it is steeped in history. There is yet another tiny priest hole (this time in the King's Room), oak-panelled rooms, and you can see the bed Charles slept in. The Charles II exhibition tells the story of his escape. We didn't join one of the free guided tours but simply wandered around on our own.

The gardens are pleasant with a nut walk and a formal knot garden. From time to time historical groups are present, displaying old-fashioned crafts and skills. We saw some Royalists and were shown how to produce a type of French Knitting using only a dolly peg.

Fact File

- ADDRESS: Boscobel House, near Albrighton, Shropshire and Moseley Old Hall, Fordhouses, Wolverhampton
- TELEPHONE: 01902 850244 (Boscobel), 01902 782808 (Moseley)
- WEBSITE: www.english-heritage.org.uk and www.nationaltrust.org.uk
- DIRECTIONS: For Boscobel, M54 to junction 3, then the A41 towards Newport. On an unclassified road between the A41 and A5. Moseley is 2 miles from junction 2 of the M54
- PUBLIC TRANSPORT: None
- DISTANCE: 20 miles
- TRAVEL TIME: 30 minutes
- OPENING: Boscobel 10.00am-5.15pm daily 1 April to end November; weekends in December. Moseley 1.30pm-5.30pm 24 March to 4 November weekends, Wednesdays, Bank Holidays and following Tuesdays; Sundays November and December
- PRICES: Boscobel adults £4.40, children £2.20, family £11.00, under-5's and English Heritage members free. Moseley adults £4.10, children £1.80, £10.25 family, under-5's and National Trust members free
- RESTAURANT FACILITIES: Yes, April to September
- NAPPY CHANGING FACILITIES: Yes, Moseley only
- HIGH CHAIRS: Yes
- DOGS: No
- PUSHCHAIR-FRIENDLY: No
- NEARBY: You can walk to White Ladies Priory from Boscobel

Ludlow Castle

Come you home of Monday
When Ludlow market hums

LUDLOW CASTLE IS A MOTTE AND BAILEY CASTLE, DATING BACK to the late 11th century. It was enlarged and modified in the 14th and 15th centuries and is an excellent example of its type. It is situated right in the centre of Ludlow on the border of England and Wales, in the most picturesque countryside. With walls to scramble on, spiral stairs to climb, and turrets to scale it provides a super venue for good days out with the kids.

As you enter the vast Outer Bailey you get an impression of space and it provides a wonderful opportunity for children who have been cooped up in a car to run about in safety. You also get an excellent view here of the main castle buildings.

This castle is today what you might call a "safe ruin". Young children can wander relatively freely, although there are some rough walls and drops into the dried-out moat. The buildings inside the Inner Bailey, including the Keep, Great Chamber and chapel are all accessible and there are still towers

"We peered out of arrow slits and narrow windows checking that no enemies were approaching"

to be climbed. From the top there are incredible views of the surrounding countryside.

The children found the castle ideal for exploration and adventure and had great fun playing hide and seek between the various rooms. (The best places to hide were in the old fireplaces.) Agile children usually have an advantage over unfit adults though as they can escape through window gaps as well as

doorways. Some areas are rather dark and children need to be watched in these sections. Generally it was no problem and our four-year-old was very happy marching up dark staircases to see what was round the next corner!

It's easy for children to gain an impression of why castles were originally built. We peered out of arrow slits and narrow windows checking that no enemies were approaching. We imagined what might have been cooked in the large furnaces which can still be seen in the Tudor Bakery, and we peered and shouted down the old well to hear our echoes.

Before leaving the castle to visit the town be sure to walk along the outside of the castle walls to get an attacker's eye view of this splendid fortress. It doesn't take long and provides another very different impression of life in a castle.

New refreshment facilities are planned in 2001 and there is a new extensive gift shop. Anyway, you are bang in the centre of the country town with its wealth of restaurants and coffee shops. Right outside the castle entrance is the market square.

Fact File

- ADDRESS: Ludlow Castle, Ludlow, Shropshire
- TELEPHONE: 01584 873355/873947
- DIRECTIONS: A4117 from Kidderminster, which is junction 4 off M5
- PUBLIC TRANSPORT: Train from Birmingham to Shrewsbury. Change at Shrewsbury for Ludlow
- DISTANCE: 50 miles
- TRAVEL TIME: 2 hours
- OPENING: Daily 10.00am-5.00pm (to 4.00pm October to April inclusive, and to 7.00pm in August). Last admission half an hour before closing. Weekends only in January
- PRICES: Adults £3.00, children £1.50, under-6's free. Family ticket £8.50
- RESTAURANT FACILITIES: In Ludlow
- NAPPY CHANGING FACILITIES: No
- HIGH CHAIRS: No
- DOGS: Yes
- PUSHCHAIR-FRIENDLY: Yes, but backpack recommended
- NEARBY: Historic Ludlow town itself. The Clee Hill for walks

Shugborough Farm & Estate

Plan on spending a full day at Shugborough — there's a Georgian farm to potter around, the Staffordshire County Museum to nose into, and an ancestral house. All of this is surrounded by glorious gardens and parkland, so that the main problem is deciding where to go first and having enough time to do it all.

You approach along a two-mile drive, passing beautiful rhododendrons which are marvellous in Spring. At the fork in the road you have to make the major decision of the day, where to go first? We chose the farm, where we found life and the daily routines of a small Georgian farm estate re-created. It is a working farm, but everyone working there is in 18th century costume: milkmaids, the miller, farmers' wives and the farmers themselves. You can walk around, see everything going on, chat to the people, and even get a chance to join in too. We baked bread in the old kitchen, got

"We baked bread in the old kitchen, got splattered by butter whilst patting the dough, and saw cheesemaking in action"

splattered by butter whilst patting the dough, and saw cheesemaking in action.

The mill wheel was a real hit with our children: the water turning the huge wheels and cogs, with the flour coming out the other end, to be used in the bakery further on. Above the mill is a museum area, where there are hands-on games to find out more about farming. Facts about crops and livestock farming are cunningly presented to children in superlarge magnetic games of worms and ladders.

☞

Hand milking can be seen each day at 4.00pm, but equally entertaining was the wooden cow which is set up in the byre for youngsters to try their own hand at milking.

There are plenty of animals to admire including pigs, geese and cows. The enclosures are well laid-out and small children can view most of them easily. There are also some more unusual features, such as a rabbit burrow, a dovecote and an observation bee hive. At the back of the courtyard is the old duck pond where you'll find an excellent picnic area and playground. Plenty of tables are available, it is well-fenced and has modern play equipment. There is a small cafe selling basic snacks.

Once we'd finished at the farm, we went up to the main estate buildings. It is a five-minute walk between them. The Mansion House, Servants' Quarters and Staffordshire County Museum are here. The mansion is the home of Lord Lichfield, and he is often to be seen on the estate: we saw him driving a mini tractor. The house is very beautiful and provides an ideal introduction to young children in visiting historical homes as the tour does not take very long (about 45 minutes). You can wander round unguided, and admire the fine furniture, paintings and ceramics. The children found the Servants' Quarters and Staffordshire County Museum more interesting, particularly the kitchen with its spread of food (tasting available), working brewery (no tasting yet!), and the hands-on washing in the laundry. They also enjoyed the carriages in the Coach House and the schoolroom.

From the Museum you can follow the Lady Walk down to the River Sow, and wander along the banks admiring the terraced lawns and ornamental gardens. The park is extensive, but well-served with paths that are easily passable for pushchairs. Dotted about are follies and monuments.

There are loads of special events throughout the year, ranging from pig handling days to village fairs, and from country dancing to country crafts. Many of these have an historical theme and would be appealing to families.

Fact File

- ADDRESS: Shugborough Park Farm, Milford, near Stafford, Staffordshire
- TELEPHONE: 01889 881388
- WEBSITE: www.nationaltrust.org.uk
- DIRECTIONS: On the A513 between Stafford and Lichfield. Junctions 13 or 14 from the M6 to Stafford
- PUBLIC TRANSPORT: None
- DISTANCE: 20 miles
- TRAVEL TIME: 45 minutes
- OPENING: Daily, except Mondays, 11.00am-5.00pm from 31 March to 30 September. Sundays only in October
- PRICES: £2.00 per vehicle, plus all-in ticket £9.00 adults, £6.00 children, under-5's free, family £22.00. Separate admission available for individual attractions. National Trust members free entry to House
- RESTAURANT FACILITIES: Yes
- NAPPY CHANGING FACILITIES: Yes
- HIGH CHAIRS: Yes
- DOGS: Park only
- PUSHCHAIR-FRIENDLY: Yes
- NEARBY: Cannock Chase (woodland common area)

Stokesay Castle

FOR A FUN INTRODUCTION TO MEDIEVAL LIFE COME TO Stokesay, a 13th century manor house built on several floors, complete with projecting timbers, shutters and ancient panelling. Note that inside there are steep stairs, not suitable for a pushchair.

There are three buildings to explore: the castle itself, a church, and a gatehouse. The church is outside the main castle complex with no charge for admission, although donations are requested. The gatehouse, through which you enter the castle, is impressively timbered. It contains the gift shop.

Once inside the castle you come first to the courtyard, a grassy area with plenty of room for running around, which has a covered well in the centre. The children made a bee-line for the well and peered in. The courtyard has plenty of benches around the outside and makes a sheltered spot to linger. The children, though, will be eager to start investigating the castle interior.

"Stokesay is still recognisable as having been a home, and provides many talking points for children"

We started our tour in the great vaulted hall, described as a church by one of our children. It is as large as a church, but it's easier to imagine more raucous activities going on here than in a church! From there the children led the way, up and down steps, into the kitchen and out again, then up and down some more steps. You'll need to supervise carefully, as many of the stairs are steep and there are open windows.

One of the joys is that Stokesay is still recognisable as having been a home, and provides many talking points for children. We asked our kids what they thought one of the recesses in the wall might have been used for. "To put their T-shirts in" came back the reply. They were also fascinated by the fact that you could see the sky up the chimney from the fireplace.

You can go round the castle with a taped tour and walkman (free). Both adults' and children's versions are provided. The child's is suitable for children from about 5-years-old. The adult version provides explanations of the architecture of the castle, whereas the child's deals more with the people who would have lived in the castle. It features Laurence of Ludlow, a wool trader who reputedly enjoyed his great feasts and entertainment in the castle. It really helps to bring the visit to life. Most weekends in the school holidays you will find Living History events going on too – games, stories and demonstrations – and we liked the sound of medieval dressing-up days.

Having been in all of the rooms in the castle, it was picnic time. You can picnic in the courtyard, or we found tables in a grassy area just outside the castle. Refreshments provided in the castle grounds are limited to home-made cakes, soup and sandwiches, with ice creams and drinks also available. Across the road from the castle, though, near the car park, there is a more extensive tea room.

Picnic over, there was more exploring to be done, and races to be raced. At last, tired, happy and heads full of history we set off home.

Fact File

- ADDRESS: Stokesay Castle, Craven Arms, Shropshire
- TELEPHONE: 01588 672544
- WEBSITE: www.english-heritage.org.uk
- DIRECTIONS: From Kidderminster take the A456, and then A4117 towards Ludlow. Off the A49 between Church Stretton and Ludlow
- PUBLIC TRANSPORT: Midland Red West 435 from Shrewsbury to Ludlow stops nearby (01345 056785)
- DISTANCE: 50 miles
- TRAVEL TIME: 1 hour
- OPENING: Daily 10.00am-6.00pm 1 April to 30 September. Wednesday-Sunday only October to March 10.00am-4.00pm
- PRICES: Adults £4.00, children £2.00, under-5's and English Heritage members free. Family £10.00
- RESTAURANT FACILITIES: Yes
- NAPPY CHANGING FACILITIES: No
- HIGH CHAIRS: No
- DOGS: No
- PUSHCHAIR-FRIENDLY: Limited
- NEARBY: Wenlock Edge, for peaceful and scenic countryside

Warwick Castle

DESCRIBED AS "THE FINEST MEDIEVAL CASTLE IN ENGLAND", as far as children are concerned Warwick Castle might have jumped straight out of a story book. Its towers, ramparts and turrets are magnificent, and the castle is a sizeable enough to get to grips with, whilst still allowing you to walk round. Arrive early, as it is very popular, and there is plenty to see.

The castle buildings are very well-preserved and embrace over 1000 years of building activity, from the original Norman mound, through the extensive medieval walls and gatehouse, the Tudor ghost tower, and the 17th and 18th century great hall and staterooms. Access to some of them is quite narrow, so be prepared to leave buggies outside and carry very young children. The leaflet with advice for visitors with pushchairs is a helpful touch.

The dungeon was our first port of call. It is dark, small, and hot, but the kids were impressed by the cage body suit. It gets busy, so be prepared to queue or go early. Alongside is the 'Death and Glory'

"Incredibly life-like figures, with sounds, sights and smells to vividly re-create all the drama of the time"

armoury exhibition, where the kids can try on helmets, pull a longbow or wield a Medieval sword.

Well worth the effort is the visit to the ramparts. There are 198 steps from top to bottom, give or take a stumble, so don't try to carry a very young child. Toddlers would need really to be on reins. Although tired at the end our 4-year-old managed it. You are rewarded for your effort with splendid views of the surrounding countryside.

If you can't face all those steps, try the Ghost Tower for size. It is smaller, and has a bedroom and study inside. Our children were suitably awed by the

recreated story.

Don't miss the Kingmaker exhibition in the Undercroft. This portrays brilliantly and graphically how Richard Neville, Earl of Warwick, prepared for battle in 1471. It has incredibly life-like figures, with sounds, sights and smells to vividly re-create all the drama of the time.

Escape out to the extensive and relatively peaceful grounds, which provide plenty of scope for letting off steam. There are wild woods and fields, formal rose gardens, bridges and an island to explore. You'll find plenty of choices for picnic spots, but be prepared to share with the roaming peacocks who are very persistent. Food snacks and ice creams are available all around the site, and in the summer you can even buy picnic boxes.

There is something on in the grassy courtyard most summer weekends. We listened to Elizabethan musicians singing and playing, and their lilting music really added to the atmosphere. There are plenty of benches where you can wait and muse while other members of the family explore more far-flung buildings. Lots of other costumed characters wander around – a rat catcher, and several courtly ladies were there on our visit. A photogenic medieval knight on horseback spends time in the grounds most days. The castle has its own resident jousting team, and on some days (particularly July and August) you can watch jousting displays on River Island, medieval games and birds of prey displays.

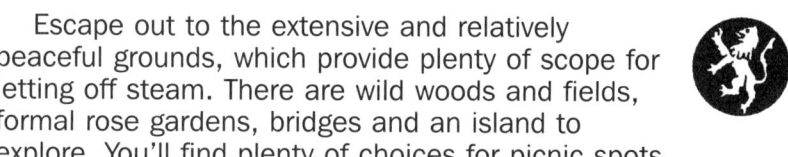

Fact File

- ADDRESS: Warwick Castle, Warwick, Warwickshire
- TELEPHONE: 01926 495421
- WEBSITE: www.warwick-castle.co.uk
- DIRECTIONS: 2 miles from junction 15 of the M40. Signposted
- PUBLIC TRANSPORT: Train from Birmingham and a 10-minute walk from the town centre
- DISTANCE: 20 miles
- TRAVEL TIME: 35 minutes
- OPENING: Daily 10.00am-6.00pm (April to October) or 5.00pm (November to March)
- PRICES: Adults £11.50, children £6.75, family £30.00, under-4's free. Reduced prices September to May
- RESTAURANT FACILITIES: Yes
- NAPPY CHANGING FACILITIES: Yes
- HIGH CHAIRS: Yes
- DOGS: No
- PUSHCHAIR-FRIENDLY: Yes
- NEARBY: Stratford on Avon

Up, Down, There & Back

Great Central Railway

CHUFF, CHUFF, CHUFF, CHUFF, WHOO, WHOO! YOU WON'T BE disappointed with a day out at the Great Central Railway. There's much more to do here than just a ride on a train and you'll have a great day.

There are four stations along the line: Loughborough, Quorn, Rothley and Leicester. The journey from Loughborough to Leicester takes about 30 minutes, but you can get on and off at any station for a nose about, which children may find as fascinating as the ride itself.

Starting at Quorn (the best arrival point if you have a pushchair as you can cross the line without having to negotiate any steps) our boys had great fun climbing onto a traction engine and pulling the levers. From there we climbed some steep steps into the 19th century signal box, which has an old-fashioned telephone, desk and typewriter. The real excitement comes from being able to pull on the levers and watch as the signal outside goes up and down. For any child who has ever wanted to be a train driver this is a chance to fulfil dreams! Back down at ground level there is a small engine placed in the station yard for children (and mums and dads) to climb into. Here you can really play at being Casey Jones.

"For any child who has ever wanted to be a train driver this is a chance to fulfil dreams!"

Next it was time to cross the line. Stop, look and listen are the instructions on the gate, but for added safety there is someone who will tell you when it is alright to cross. We were now on the platform itself, recreated to the 1940's, and with a station master's bunker and NAAFI. There is also a LNER carriage, home to an enthralling model railway, where you can see Thomas and Percy and Henry and James going round and round, under bridges, into the station, through the tunnels and back out again.

The first real train arrived with a hissing of steam and a very loud chuff, chuff. So off we went to Loughborough, where a Thomas the Tank Engine day was in full steam. Thomas was ferrying eager young and not-so-young enthusiasts for a short journey within the station yard, the Fat Controller was shouting his instructions, and Rupert Bear paraded up and down shaking hands and giving hugs. Although this was a special event day, on a normal day there is still lots to see.

Cross the track to visit the locomotive sheds and see renovation work being carried out on some of the engines. It's very cramped in here, but we managed to get through with the pushchair. The air inside the sheds is filled with oil and grease, and as you walk between the huge locos you get a real sense of their power: our eldest commented that the wheels were taller than daddy. Outside the sheds, we watched as one of the engines was given a drink. It was a very thirsty engine: it drank gallons before hissing into life and setting off on its next trip.

At Loughborough there is a gift shop, full of Thomas the Tank Engine memorabilia, and a station buffet. On the special day when we visited there was also a hot dog and candy floss stall and swing boat rides for children. If you fancy something more peaceful Quorn has a small picnic area. If you've time, do the round trip to Leicester and back. There's not much at Leicester, and Rothley is similar to Quorn, except that its signal box can't be visited. Nevertheless, it makes a treat to steam through the countryside at the end of the day.

Fact File

● ADDRESS: Great Central Station, Loughborough, Leicestershire
● TELEPHONE: 01509 230726
● WEBSITE: www.gcrailway.co.uk
● DIRECTIONS: M42 northbound, A42 to junction 13, and A512 to Loughborough. Once at Loughborough turn right at the 2nd roundabout, signposted A6 Leicester, and follow the brown tourist signs to Quorn station
● PUBLIC TRANSPORT: Train to Loughborough and 15-minute walk to Great Central Station. Or train to Leicester and short bus ride to Leicester North Station
● DISTANCE: 45 miles
● TRAVEL TIME: 1 hour
● OPENING: Daily beginning June to end September; weekends and Bank Holidays the rest of the year. Trains from 9.30am weekends, 11.00am weekdays (from Loughborough)
● PRICES: Round trip adults £9.50, children £6.50, family £19.50, under-3's free. Extra on special event days
● RESTAURANT FACILITIES: Yes
● NAPPY CHANGING FACILITIES: No
● HIGH CHAIRS: No
● DOGS: Yes
● PUSHCHAIR-FRIENDLY: Yes
● NEARBY: Nottingham Heritage Centre (0115 940 5705), 7 miles north of Loughborough

The Gloucestershire & Warwickshire Railway

AHH, YOU CAN'T BEAT THE WHIFF OF COAL, STEAM AND ENGINE oil in the nostrils! Both big and small lovers of steam trains will get a nose-full of nostalgia here, as well as plenty to look at and steam rides through glorious Cotswold countryside. Originally part of the Great Western Railway, six and a half miles of track have been re-laid and restored since the Railway's demise in the late 1970's. Running from Toddington to Gotherington it is a round trip of 13 miles, taking about an hour station to station.

We started off at Toddington on a busy Vintage Steam Gala weekend, with many other people and cats-and-dogs worth of rain. Despite the crowds and the weather we managed to leap into an empty compartment almost immediately, pulled by the suitably impressively sighing and groaning Dumbleton Hall steam engine (big, black, circa 1929 beast to non-train spotters). With a blast

"With a blast of the whistle and a wave of the flag we were off"

of the whistle and a wave of the flag we were off, past the signal box, loco warehouses and finally the fields and trees of the open countryside. There are pretty villages to see on the way, bridges to cross, remains of a 13th century Cistercian Abbey ("like a dragon's castle"), and for the really observant, remnants of a medieval farming system ("a bit like a giant's lilo").

At Winchcombe you can get out to visit the signal box and see the renovation sheds full of carriages and wagons in various states of repair, before the train takes a deep breath and hauls itself up to the

mouth of the tunnel. Wheee! it's a long one, and was the highlight of the day for our crew. It's on then to Gotherington where you can't get out but can watch from your carriage as the engine is switched round to the other end of the train for the return journey.

Back at Toddington there was plenty to see and do on our visit, with steam fire engines, steam rollers, traction engines, motorcycles and fairground organs in full voice. All was bustle and noise and dripping steam. We particularly enjoyed the model display which ranged from steam engines to dolls' houses and from fairground rides to narrow boats. On non-Gala days there are still the signal box, running shed – a sort of garage for steam locomotives – and the engine repair workshops (although access is limited). On occasional summer

Sundays there is a narrow gauge railway which offers 15-minute round trips.

The station cafe; the Flag and Whistle, has reasonably priced snacks and cakes, or there are picnic areas at both Toddington and Winchcombe. Winchcombe itself is a pretty town, about a mile's walk from the station. For a busy day try a visit here during the Steam Gala in mid-October (check for exact dates), one of the diesel galas or Thomas the Tank days. Other days it will be quieter, but no less rewarding.

Fact File

● ADDRESS: The Gloucestershire & Warwickshire Railway, Toddington Station, near Cheltenham, Gloucestershire
● TELEPHONE: 01242 621405
● WEBSITE: www.gwsr.plc.uk
● DIRECTIONS: M5 junction 9, A46 towards Evesham then B4077 towards Stow. Go through Toddington and follow signs to railway
● PUBLIC TRANSPORT: Coach services by Castleways (01242 602949)
● DISTANCE: 55 miles
● TRAVEL TIME: 1 hour 30 minutes
● OPENING: 11.00am-5.30pm weekends and Bank Holidays from beginning of April to end of October. Diesel only Sundays in January, February and November
● PRICES: Round trip adults £7.00, children £4.00, family £19.00, under-5's free
● NAPPY CHANGING FACILITIES: No
● HIGH CHAIRS: No
● RESTAURANT FACILITIES: Yes
● DOGS: Yes
● PUSHCHAIR-FRIENDLY: Yes
● NEARBY: Sudeley Castle (01242 603197)

Llangollen Wharf & Steam Railway

All was a-shake and a-shiver, glints and gleams and sparkles, rustle and swirl, chatter and bubbles

FORGET THE TRAFFIC JAMS AS THE A5 ENTERS THE WELSH Mountains, and make a trip to Llangollen for an opportunity to step back in time to see how people coped with getting out and about a century ago. With its horse-drawn canal boat rides and steam railway Llangollen is a treat for transport freaks.

Make your way down to the river as you arrive in the town. You'll see the train station next to Castle Street Bridge, and the canal boat rides operate from the wharf above the station. Look out for the blackboards down by the bridge giving times of the boats running that day. To get up to the canal is a steep short climb by steps or ramped pathway, or you can access it by road.

"With its open sides and covered roof the old-fashioned narrow boat is ideal if it is rainy"

Once up there you are straight onto the towpath with toddlers needing watching by the open canal.

We were lucky, hopping immediately onto a boat, pushchair and all. There was plenty of room, and the kids stood on the bench seats spotting the huge perch and roach streaming past. Other thrills were meeting another boat coming the other way (yes, there is room), the tunnel, and the fishermen on the towpath who caught an enormous fish just as we passed.

The horse pulls you along under the trees at slow walking pace through stunning upland scenery to

Pentrefelin and back. The entire return trip lasts 45 minutes – just the right length to maintain interest. With its open sides and covered roof the old-fashioned narrow boat is ideal if it is rainy.

Horse-drawn canal trips run frequently throughout the day. If you just miss one, spend the waiting time making friends with the horses kept in small stable boxes alongside the Centre. Alternatively, try the cakes on offer in the tearoom, and admire the view over the town from the outside terrace.

Real enthusiasts may want to try the 2-hour trip from the Wharf to Froncysyllte aquaduct on the Thomas Telford narrow boat. Fantastic views, a castle to admire, and the dizzying 126'-high aquaduct are on offer (advisable to book in advance).

From May to October steam trains run hourly from the Victorian station below the Wharf, but check times in advance. The return trip up to Carrog takes about 1 hour 20 minutes. The train steams up into the mountains in restored carriages, giving a real taste of what life was like in 'the old days'. After stopping at Berwyn with great views of the river Dee rushing below there is a long pull through a very dark tunnel.

☞ We got out at the beautiful 1950's station at Carrog and inspected the engine. Although described as medium-sized by the driver it looked enormous to us: all shining black coachwork, gleaming trim and enough hisses, puffs and whistles to enthral any Thomas the Tank enthusiast. You can get up onto the footplate, where we discovered that the driver actually owned the train himself, and the kids were impressed by the roaring fire and the suitably-grimy fireman, in fact a woman.

From Carrog there is a good footpath walk. Or there is a picnic spot and play area next to the platform at Glyndyfrdwy and you can get off there too and watch the comings and goings.

Back at Llangollen have a look around. It is distinctly Welsh with plenty of souvenir shops, tearooms and intriguing signposts and street names. There is a small Victorian school museum and riverbank walks and picnic spots.

Fact File

- ADDRESS: Horse Drawn Boat Centre, The Wharf, Llangollen, Clwyd. Steam Railway, The Station, Abbey Road, Llangollen, Clwyd
- TELEPHONE: 01978 860702 (canal boats), 01978 860951/860979 (railway)
- WEBSITE: www.horsedrawnboats.co.uk and www.llangollen-railway.co.uk
- DIRECTIONS: M6/M54, then A5 to Shrewsbury and on to Llangollen
- PUBLIC TRANSPORT: Nearest mainline trains are 5 miles away at Ruabon. Buses from Wrexham and Ruabon hourly
- DISTANCE: 75 miles
- TRAVEL TIME: 1 hour 45 minutes
- OPENING: Canal boats daily from Easter to October 11.00am-5.00pm. Railway daily from May to October, Easter week and half-terms; weekends rest of year (except November, January and February)
- PRICES: Boats £3.50 adults, £2.50 children, £5.00 one adult with one child, under-3's free. Railway return trip £7.50 adults, £3.80 children, £18.00 family, under 4's free
- RESTAURANT FACILITIES: Yes
- NAPPY CHANGING FACILITIES: Yes
- HIGH CHAIRS: No
- DOGS: Yes
- PUSHCHAIR-FRIENDLY: Yes
- NEARBY: Dr Who exhibition and Motor Museum in Llangollen

Severn Valley Railway

*The Engineer said he rang the bell
And she blew, Whoo-oo-oo!*

WHOLE TRAINS, BITS OF TRAINS, SMARTLY PAINTED TRAINS AND rusty shells of trains greet you as you enter the station of the Severn Valley Railway in Bridgnorth. Don't be put off; it's not a scrap yard, but a store place for all the bits waiting for restoration. It's worth looking at, because when you've seen some of these bits, it makes you appreciate the finished product. What a product! The train waiting at the station was sleekly black with silver trim, towering over us and hissing steam – impressive indeed.

You can start at either Bridgnorth or Kidderminster. At Bridgnorth avoid the overflow car park if you have a pushchair, as it is a steep climb. The station is as it would have been in days gone past, with well-worn trunks and suitcases stacked on trolleys and original posters and advertisements up on the walls. You have to cross over to the other side of the track to catch the train, up and over the bridge. If you can't manage the bridge with a pushchair ask to be escorted across the track on foot.

"Noses pressed against the window, we strained to see the man with the green flag"

Once aboard we sat back to enjoy the journey, whilst the children stood with noses pressed against the window, straining to see the man with the green flag. They weren't disappointed: we'd sat next to the guard's van and he obligingly stood right outside our window, waved his flag, blew his whistle and we were off with a "clickety, clack, clickety, clack".

The journey from Bridgnorth to Kidderminster takes just over an hour, stopping at four stations on route, all pretty as a picture with lovingly tended flower beds. At Kidderminster there are the usual facilities, a railway museum crammed with railway memorabilia, a mini railway giving rides and a replica of a lever frame signal box which kids can play with to their hearts' content.

The return ticket allows you unlimited travel, so you can get on or off at any of the stations. Toilets are at all stations and on all trains, and both Kidderminster and Bridgnorth have nappy changing facilities. There are refreshments on most trains and at Kidderminster, Bewdley and Bridgnorth. There are model railways at both Bewdley and Hampton Loade. At Highley you can picnic in the Severn Valley Country Park and wander down to the river – ask for the Country Park halt and flag down the next train when you want to return. Be prepared for fairly steep hills if you do explore further afield, as the railway runs through the steep-sided Severn Valley.

We got off at Arley and walked down to the river to watch the canoes going back and forth under the bridge below us. There is also a pub 100 yards from Arley station, with a beer garden and farm animals. An alternative stop would be Hampton Loade, where you can get a ferry across the river to a pub for 20p.

Fact File

- ADDRESS: The Railway Station, Bridgnorth, Shropshire
- TELEPHONE: 01299 403816, Talking Timetable 01299 401001
- WEBSITE: www.svr.co.uk
- DIRECTIONS: For Kidderminster follow the signs southbound from the M5 junction 3, or northbound from junction 6. For Bridgnorth, turn right off the A458 Stourbridge to Bridgnorth road onto the A442 signposted Low Town and follow signs
- PUBLIC TRANSPORT: Kidderminster Station is adjacent to the mainline station, with frequent services from Birmingham or Worcester. Midland Red bus from Wolverhampton to Bridgnorth
- DISTANCE: 15 miles (Kidderminster), 25 miles (Bridgnorth)
- TRAVEL TIME: 30-45 minutes
- OPENING: Daily May to beginning October; holiday periods and weekends the rest of the year. Check timetables in advance
- PRICES: Adults £9.60, £4.80 children, or family £23.00 for unlimited travel on day. Under-5's free
- RESTAURANT FACILITIES: Yes
- NAPPY CHANGING FACILITIES: Yes
- HIGH CHAIRS: No
- DOGS: Yes
- PUSHCHAIR-FRIENDLY: Yes
- NEARBY: Rays Farm Country Matters (01299 841255) at Bridgnorth

The Sun Has Got His Hat On

Beeston Castle

She marched them up to the top of the hill . . .

PEPPERING THE COUNTRYSIDE OF CHESHIRE ARE A NUMBER OF castles left behind by the Normans, used for defence in further skirmishes, battered by the British climate and plundered and vandalised through the centuries. Like Beeston, now owned by English Heritage, many are at last being lovingly tended by their keepers. The armies that turn out today carry cameras, binoculars, butty boxes and disposable nappies. Our's did, anyway. And it was something of a battle to reach the summit of Beeston's well chosen hill. I felt as though I was wearing chain-mail body stocking as we forged onwards and upwards to reach our conquest. But it was worth it. Pack up the picnic, get your stout walking shoes, root out the kids' kite and take a deep breath.

"The armies that turn out today carry cameras, binoculars, butty boxes and disposable nappies"

At the entrance at the bottom of the hill is a souvenir shop and museum with archaeological finds and information. You can get hot drinks and snacks from the vending machine here, and it's a good idea to use the toilets here too as there are none in the castle itself. At peak visiting times there's a hot dog van in the car park but come prepared in case of disappointment.

We took the middle path up the hill and stopped for a breather on a thoughtfully-provided bench, after about 15 minutes. Here you will see that a path has been trodden either side and these both lead to the remains at the top. If you take the left you'll find the going a bit easier. In our ignorance of this we didn't and it was a good half hour before we arrived panting at the drawbridge.

Looking down you can see the old stone ramp which used to meet a small wooden bridge. Now there is a newer bridge, leading onto the plateau where the rocky ground is bordered by what's left of the castle walls. Don't try to get the buggy round *this* crazy paving, and hold onto those toddlers! It was a blustery day when we braved this trip and up on top the wind gusted round. There are rooms to walk into, from whose slitted arrow holes you can survey the green and brown land that men through history have scrutinised for signs of danger. Look out for rare Peregrine falcons helping to guard the craggy tops, or nesting ravens. The scenery from the Castle is glorious and if you look over the bridge a neighbouring fort can be seen. Imagine what must have gone on in the valley between!

We made our way back down the outer pathway, passing look out points, pieces of wall and steps. We even came across a very old well which has a tree growing from one of its sides. The raw, unfussed nature of Beeston is invigorating and you can see the original craftsmanship in the remains, filling in the gaps of time with your imagination. There's no one to frown at little tourists as they trespass on lawns and touch exhibits. You can shout, scamper about, run and jump, throw tantrums and whine for more chocolate as much as you like. We did!

At the bottom we congratulated ourselves, checked the suspension on the push-chair and purchased supplies from the shop. There is a flatter grassy area here with benches, ideal for picnics. Nearby are some caves, which you can reach by sliding down a wilderness (as our 7-year-old did) or by walking down some steps. Their entrances are railed off but it's quite something to press your forehead against the bars and stare into the darkness. The children were wary about bears so we continued our walk, searching for dinosaur fossils and mammoth tusks, arrow heads and wild boar.

Fact File

- ADDRESS: Beeston Castle, Beeston, Cheshire
- TELEPHONE: 01829 260464
- WEBSITE: www.english-heritage.org.uk
- DIRECTIONS: Junction 16 off M6, follow A500 to Natwich, and the A534 west to the A49 Chester to Whitchurch road. Just off the A49 in the Chester direction
- PUBLIC TRANSPORT: None
- DISTANCE: 50 miles
- TRAVEL TIME: 1 hour
- OPENING: Daily 10.00am-6.00pm (summer), 10.00am-4.00pm (winter)
- PRICES: Adults £2.90, children £1.50, under-5's free. English Heritage members free. Extra charge for special event days
- RESTAURANT FACILITIES: No
- NAPPY CHANGING FACILITIES: Yes
- HIGH CHAIRS: No
- DOGS: Yes
- PUSHCHAIR-FRIENDLY: Just about
- NEARBY: Stapeley Water Gardens (01270 628628) Nantwich for The Palms tropical oasis gardens

The Birmingham Botanical Gardens

A VISIT TO SOME GARDENS MAY NOT MEET WITH MUCH enthusiasm with many children but the Botanical Gardens in Birmingham will change all that. Ideal for a picnic and run around, they are really easy to get to, being very near the city centre in a leafy suburb, and give a haven from the hurly burly of city life.

Start off in the glasshouses for an immediate impression of a tropical wilderness and the chance to play spot the banana – our kids loved seeing which way they grow. Be prepared to dodge a few sprinklers at watering time: we got wet, which added to the hilarity. The most amazing plants in these houses captured the interest of our children on the spot. We spied cotton, dates, citrus fruits and loofahs to name but a few. During the summer months many of these are in fruit which means children can recognise them for themselves.

On leaving the glasshouses you enter a wonderfully laid-out park which provides a super environment for a family day out playing hide and seek between the trees, or

"We spied cotton, dates, citrus fruits and loofahs to name but a few"

just ambling around the paths. Even on a busy Sunday afternoon it did not feel crowded. Children are able to play at will on the lawns and along the paths without restrictions. The waterfall and pool area are fenced off to children but a gate gives access to adults.

For older children there is an orienteering course set out in the park. They are given a map and have to find their way between marker posts. At each post they collect a stamp and a full card of stamps

receives a certificate at the end. Quite demanding at times, this is an excellent way to provide older children with something specific to do while in the park. For all children, the adventure playground trail is very good and provides an extra opportunity for them to let off steam. Around the park there are aviaries of exotic birds and stocks of old breeds of fowl, pheasants and doves. These make a popular diversion from plants for children.

The Pavilion cafe offers a good selection of snack meals and cakes, which you can eat either inside or out on the terrace. It overlooks the main lawn, a large natural amphitheatre containing a bandstand. On most Sunday afternoons you'll find a 30-piece Silver band playing here, which the kids will love, giving you a chance to loll on the grass whilst they scamper around.

Don't miss a visit to the Bonsai collection as you leave. There are some truly splendid examples here,

some of which are well over 100-years-old. Our children found these fascinating.

Be warned – parking at the Botanical Gardens is quite difficult. An alternative is to park on the surrounding streets.

Fact File

- ADDRESS: Botanical Gardens, Westbourne Road, Edgbaston, Birmingham
- TELEPHONE: 0121 454 1860
- WEBSITE: www.bham-bot-gdns.demon.co.uk
- DIRECTIONS: From city centre follow signs to Birmingham West and Edgbaston, then signs to Botanical Gardens
- PUBLIC TRANSPORT: Buses 10, 21, 22, 23, 29 and 103
- DISTANCE: 1 mile
- TRAVEL TIME: 10-15 minutes
- OPENING: Daily 9.00am-7.00pm or dusk (8.00pm summer weekends). Opens at 10.00am on Sundays. Last admission 30 minutes before closing
- PRICES: Adults £4.80, children £2.60, family £12.50, under-5's free
- RESTAURANT FACILITIES: Yes
- NAPPY CHANGING FACILITIES: Yes
- HIGH CHAIRS: Yes
- DOGS: No
- PUSHCHAIR-FRIENDLY: Yes
- NEARBY: City centre museums and art galleries

Broadway Tower Country Park

DON'T FORGET TO PACK YOUR SAUSAGES AND COME TO Broadway for the definitive 'Picnic with a View'. There's a choice of two walks through breathtaking countryside, a tower to climb, adventure playground, and plenty of space to run around, picnic or barbecue your own food.

As we approached Broadway (a very pretty village in its own right) we had a competition to see who could spot the Tower first. I forget who won, but it is not hard to identify, standing majestically right on the edge of the Cotswolds. A folly built in the 1700's in the midst of a picturesque and romantic landscape, it was later a holiday retreat to William Morris, and is now a country park area with plenty to offer those wanting to blow away cobwebs. It is quite exposed though, so on a windy day pack warm clothes.

"For the intrepid picnicer barbecues are provided"

Escaping from the car, the children made a beeline for the Tower. There is a stairs-up and stairs-down system to get to the top, which means it is all very orderly and no little feet get trodden on. With only 75 steps up our 5-year-old declared it 'easy-peasy climbing', but you'll want to keep hold of young ones when you get to the top, as it is a dizzy experience with a vast view. It wasn't clear enough to see the Welsh mountains on the day we visited, but apparently you can on some days, and 12 counties too.

On the way down, look in on the exhibitions of the history of the tower and William Morris, and then back outdoors again, where you'll have to decide whether to do the walk before or after your picnic and playtime.

There is choice of two walks: a straight 45-minute stroll along the ridge and back, or a longer, one hour 30 minutes' circular ramble through rolling countryside over stiles, down the slope and up again. Both are clearly marked on maps you are given on arrival, and both also form part of the Cotswold Way. Should you be feeling really energetic you could always suggest that you do the 100-odd miles on to Bath!

The longer walk can be a mite muddy in places and strenuous for those with a pushchair – you'll have to lug it over a few stiles too. However, it makes a pleasant walk, not too long for small legs, and there is always the adventure play area to bribe them with afterwards.

Back near the entrance is a hands-on farm, home to a herd of very tame red deer, goats, pigs, rabbits and chickens, plus rare breeds of Highland cattle and Cotswold sheep. Next on is the adventure area, carefully sited out of the wind in the shelter of trees. It proved fun and exciting, with all the usual equipment including aerial runway and trampoline. The suggested route was a test of stamina and strength over timber and rope, certainly not for softies but ideal for budding Gladiators.

There are several picnic areas set aside with picnic tables and superb views. For the intrepid, barbecues are provided, under cover or in the open, and charcoal is on sale at the shop. The Rookery Barn serves good hot and cold snacks too, and has a delightful terrace where you can linger whilst supervising a giant game of draughts or chess on an enormous chequered board.

Fact File

- ADDRESS: Broadway Tower Country Park, Broadway, Worcestershire
- TELEPHONE: 01386 852390
- WEBSITE: http://home.clara.net/broadway-tower
- DIRECTIONS: A435 to Evesham, then the A44 towards Stowe and Oxford. Signposted six miles south-east of Evesham
- PUBLIC TRANSPORT: Buses from Broadway, Evesham and Chipping Campden
- DISTANCE: 50 miles
- TRAVEL TIME: 1 hour 30 minutes
- OPENING: Daily Easter to end October, 10.00am-5.00pm. Tower only weekends October-March (weather permitting)
- PRICES: Adults £4.00, children £2.30, under-4's free. Family £11.50
- NAPPY CHANGING FACILITIES: Yes
- HIGH CHAIRS: Yes
- RESTAURANT FACILITIES: Yes
- DOGS: Yes, except in Tower
- PUSHCHAIR-FRIENDLY: Yes, except in Tower
- NEARBY: Broadway Teddy Bear Museum (01386 858323)

Himley Park & Hall

EXTENSIVE CAPABILITY BROWN GROUNDS, WOODS TO EXPLORE and a Hall with art exhibitions; whenever you visit Himley Park, there is always lots to enjoy.

One hot summer's day we started our visit with a walk through the pleasant shade of Himley Wood. You can either follow the path to the right of the stream or go over the small bridge and tramp through the woods to the left of the stream. Whichever route you take, have a look at the waterfall, which tumbles from the nearby lake to the stream.

Walking along the path, we stopped to look at the small lake with its abundance of lily pads, and imagined what Jeremy Fisher would have made of it as a place to catch his supper. Around the sides of the lake the willow trees hang down to the water's edge: a good source of fun for children. Ours jumped up to try and catch hold of the leaves and ran around among the branches playing their version of hide and seek (if I can't see you, you can't see me!)

"Hollow trees and huge tree stumps provide a great playground"

We made our way back through the undergrowth of Himley Wood. Here the ivy trails along the ground, making a beautiful green carpet and the hollow trees and huge tree stumps provide a great playground.

If you are feeling adventurous climb up the hill at the back of the Hall and follow the path along the top of the hill, leading back eventually to the large lake at the far end of the park. It's quite a climb (not recommended with a pushchair), but beautiful in spring when the ground is covered with daffs and bluebells. "Rocket" seats carved out of tree trunks on the slopes above the lake are just great for blasting into space! The ducks on the lake are particularly obliging when it comes to feeding. They will come out of the water and eat the bread from your hand, but hold on to little children, as the lake shore slopes quite steeply.

The Park itself provides acres of play area. Even on a sweltering day, when the large car park appears bursting, it never seems crowded. Whether it be football, cricket, bowls, frisbee or rounders, there is plenty of space to play. The same goes for picnics; you won't feel as though you are sharing your patch of grass with the family next door. There are tables outside the snack bar or benches along the side of the stream, but for eating out on the grass it is a good idea to take a rug.

Calm them down with a walk round the outside of Himley Hall. Around two sides of the Hall are croquet lawns, where you may be lucky enough to catch a game to watch during the Summer. Inside, the Hall plays host to a variety of exhibitions throughout the year, including county art and glass displays. The toilets inside the Hall are far superior to those in the Park.

Many other events take place in Himley Park itself, mainly during the Summer. You can expect to see horse shows, car shows, craft fairs, model car racing, or the annual Dudley show.

Fact File

- ADDRESS: Himley Hall and Park, Himley, Dudley, West Midlands
- TELEPHONE: Himley Park 01902 324093, Hall 01902 326665
- DIRECTIONS: Signposted off the A449, 6 miles south of Wolverhampton. The entrance to the park is on the B4176
- PUBLIC TRANSPORT: Train to Wolverhampton, and bus number 256 to School Road/Stourbridge Road. 10-minute walk from there
- DISTANCE: 15 miles
- TRAVEL TIME: 45 minutes
- OPENING: Park daily, dawn to dusk. Hall from March to September, Tuesday-Saturday 12.00 noon-5.00pm, Sundays and Bank Holidays 2.00pm-5.00pm
- PRICES: Pay and Display car park £1.00 all day, Hall and park free. Admission charge for special events
- RESTAURANT FACILITIES: Snacks
- NAPPY CHANGING FACILITIES: No
- HIGH CHAIRS: No
- DOGS: Yes
- PUSHCHAIR-FRIENDLY: Yes
- NEARBY: Baggeridge Country Park

Notes

Other Books

ALSO AVAILABLE IN THE DAYS OUT WITH KIDS
SERIES:

DAYS OUT WITH KIDS in the **South East**
TRIED-AND-TESTED FUN FAMILY
OUTINGS IN KENT, SURREY, SUSSEX, HAMPSHIRE,
BERKSHIRE, ESSEX, HERTFORDSHIRE,
BEDFORDSHIRE AND BUCKINGHAMSHIRE.
166 PAGES, PAPERBACK, £5.99 ISBN 1-901411-303

DAYS OUT WITH KIDS in the **North West**
TRIED-AND-TESTED FUN FAMILY
OUTINGS IN LANCASHIRE, MERSEYSIDE,
DERBYSHIRE AND CHESHIRE.
128 PAGES, PAPERBACK, £5.99 ISBN 1-901411-32X

ALL OTHER BOOKS ARE AVAILABLE FROM BOOKSHOPS OR
DIRECT FROM:

BON•BON VENTURES
24 ENDLESHAM ROAD
LONDON SW12 8JU
TEL: 020 8488 3011   FAX: 020 8265 1700
www.daysoutwithkids.co.uk

PAYMENT MAY BE MADE BY CREDIT CARD (ACCESS/VISA/MASTERCARD), OR BY
CHEQUE /POSTAL ORDER PAYABLE TO BONBON VENTURES. PLEASE ALLOW
£1.00 POSTAGE AND PACKING FOR THE FIRST BOOK, AND 50P PER BOOK
FOR SUBSEQUENT BOOKS.

Also visit our DAYS OUT WITH KIDS website on:

www.daysoutwithkids.co.uk

It has lots of information on events at the attractions featured in
this book, special offers and recommendations for trips all
round the country. You can use it to e-mail us with your
comments on trips featured or your suggestions for new trips.
We'd love to hear from you!

Notes